The Thrill of the Ride

Sally Ben

© 2022 Sally Ben

Faithbuilders Publishing
12 Dukes Court, Bognor Road,
Chichester, PO19 8FX, United Kingdom

www.faithbuilderspublishing.com

ISBN: 978-1-913181-78-9

British Library Cataloguing in Publication Data. A catalogue record for this book is available from the British Library

Formatted by Faithbuilders Publishing
Cover by Esther Kotecha, EKDesign
Printed in the United Kingdom

Contents

Dedication

"To my best man in the whole world, who spurs me onwards and upwards."

Acknowledgement

"Grateful thanks to my friend John Hearson, who has patiently read each chapter, and offered helpful insights and amendments. He has cheered me on every step of the way, encouraging me that this is God's story written in our lives."

Chapter 1

Early Influences – Meet Sally

The walk through the cornfield

Walking in the lovely English countryside on a sunny day early in September, enjoying the bustling life of the trees and hedgerows. I come to a cornfield where the golden stalks are standing tall and proud. I need to get to the other side, but there is no obvious path, so I push my way through the tall, golden stalks to clear a way. A couple of days later, I take the same walk and come to the same cornfield – which path will I take?

The same one I pushed my way through the last time, of course.

I first heard this picture story when I was training as a life coach. It is used to illustrate how we develop thought pathways and how we tend to return to these same pathways. The line of thought can be triggered by any one of the senses, or by a memory, and off we go down the same pathway. If you could have an aerial view of the pathway you had forged, you may or may not find it was the best way through the cornfield. This is the same in the case of early influences that have developed our thought patterns.

Sally

Litter and lies

"Sweet Heaven" was the counter in the Newsagent shop that my Dad and Mum managed in the 1960s – for sixpence (pre-decimal English money), you could buy four fruit salad chews, four black jack chews, two shrimps, two aniseed balls, and a liquorice Catherine wheel! There were other delights in jars that lined the shelves of the shop, some of which are still available today – fizzy sherbet lemons; tangy pear drops; two-tone rhubarb and custard; all of which still conjure up sights, smells and tastes.

The shop was situated on a small parade at the side of a drive banked with rhododendrons. When they were in season, it was like walking through a tunnel of glorious crimsons and purples. On the other side of the drive was a large, imposing secondary school building. In the security of the shop, I was sometimes allowed to serve the older secondary school students from behind the penny sweet counter. However, outside of the shop, the authority of the secondary school teachers posed an authoritarian threat in my young mind. So, it came about that one day I left the shop walking towards the rhododendron tunnel, with a treat given as a reward for my serving behind the sweet counter. I carelessly dropped the wrapper on the ground, and was halted by a stern voice behind me: "Don't you *ever* let me see you drop litter like that again!" I shrivelled up inside as I turned to see a secondary school teacher behind me. It didn't need an "Or else I will ...", but saw me scrambling to pick up the offending paper. Not only that, but somewhere it lodged deep within my psyche, to the extent that, when I visited beautiful islands in much later years, I was appalled and quick to reprimand anyone spoiling their magnificent surroundings by throwing rubbish. It was a lifelong lesson.

It wasn't only sweets that offered temptation – one Christmas time, I looked longingly at the Christmas decorations. Again in the 1960's style, there were honeycomb tissue paper bells, crepe paper garlands, and shiny foil chains – oh, how wonderful they would look adorning my bedroom! But my Mum was adamant, they were unnecessary items when we already had decorations that would be brought down from the loft at the due time. Not to be thwarted, I devised what I thought was a clever plan. I gave my best friend my money and asked her to go into the shop and buy me the desired decorations. She was happy to oblige. However, here my cunning failed me, as I hid the decorations in my underwear drawer. You guessed it

– my Mum was the one who tidied the laundry away, and it did not take long for her to discover my treasures. All my explanations that they belonged to my friend were of course unravelled. The sting in the tail were her words that still ring sharply in my ears more than fifty years later: "It's not so much that you did it, but that you lied to me." Consequently, I still have a loathing of being lied to and have heard myself repeat her words through the years.

Pushing through

"I've got tummy ache Mum, I can't go to school."

"You get yourself off, you'll be fine when you get there, and I need to go to work."

This was a frequently repeated morning scenario in my last year of primary school, as I sat miserably at the bottom of the stairs clad in my grey pleated skirt and grey school jumper. We had moved to a new district in time for the start of the school year, and I was scared to death of my new teacher. So much so, that I would record in my diary each day: "Miss Holden in a good mood," or "Miss Holden in a bad mood." However, always desperate to be in people's good books, I had my strategies. Miss Holden was a talented seamstress and artist – sadly, two skills that have always eluded me – but "words" are more my forte. I would see my opportunity and grasp it – "I like your dress, Miss Holden," or "That is a lovely colour on you, Miss Holden." I survived the year, and learnt the lesson that you had to be dying not to go to school in our house! My Dad and Mum were grafters, and their example left a lasting impression on me to work hard at whatever I do in life.

"Not good enough"

Snow! So exciting, and such a rare occurrence in the south of England, especially when it kept falling and painted our world in a shiny, crystallised white. I don't remember building a snowman with coal eyes and a carrot nose, or joining in a passionate snowball fight, but I do remember getting a yard broom and a garden spade to try to clear the garden path. It was hard work, and my fingers and toes were stinging from the cold when I finally went back indoors to strip off my soggy gloves and socks. But as I cradled a steaming mug of hot chocolate, I also had a warm inner glow, thinking of how pleased my Dad would be on his return from work. Today, added to his responsibilities as an area manger now of a number of newsagent shops, he would also have faced the fatigue of driving in the treacherous snowy conditions.

Dad returned safe but weary, and tucked into the dinner my Mum had put to one side and then warmed up for him over a pan of boiling water (no such luxury as a microwave in those days!). No reference was made to the cleared path. No comment forthcoming. But none was necessary, when soon after dinner he went out and cleared the path again himself. The message was clear, what I had done was "Not good enough".

This same message became like the groove in an old scratched vinyl record, where it gets stuck and plays over and over again. Running home from school, bubbling over with excitement, to proudly announce that I had come fifth in the class exams. My Dad's response, "Well you didn't come top, did you?" I wasn't good enough for him, I missed his mark. Doing a twirl in a prized new dress, desperately longing for my Dad's approval, wanting to know I was beautiful in his sight. Yet again my confidence bubble burst, when he glanced up over the top of his newspaper, and said, "Yes, it's alright." Much later in life, I came to realise that this was one of my poor thought pathways, that had to be reprogrammed, or it would costly me dearly.

Dreams and challenges

The letter with my name on it had arrived. It had the logo on it of White Lodge, the Royal Ballet School in London. As I held it in my hands, all my dreams passed before my eyes. Margot Fonteyn, the prima ballerina, was my heroine, and in my mind's eye I could see myself, as I had seen her, floating across the stage in the ballet Swan Lake.

It had been with a mixture of excitement and trepidation that I had travelled with my Mum up to London, the big city, to attend the first audition. White Lodge is a Georgian House situated in Richmond Park and it was challenging enough walking up the grandiose staircase towards the changing room. Then, with not a hair out of place, I had danced in front of an austere panel of Royal Ballet staff.

Imagine my amazement and delight, when I was told that I had passed to the next stage, which involved another trip to London for a gruelling dance session and a medical. Now, with trembling hands, I opened the letter that held the answer to the pathway into my future. At eleven years old, was this homing pigeon ready to join boarding school with the dancing elite? I really wasn't sure. So as I read the words, "We are sorry to tell you that you have been **unsuccessful**...", I don't quite know which was greater – my disappointment, or my relief.

Dancing, like many other disciplines, involves strenuous training, week in and week out. The commitment is not only required of the dancer, but also of the long suffering parents, who provide the finance for lessons, exam fees, competitions and costumes, along with accompaniment and transport. As a young girl I used to ask my Dad, "Do you love me?" His regular retort was, "Of course I love you, I give you lifts to dancing lessons don't I?" This was not the response I longed for, but in hindsight, when I am now asked to be the proverbial taxi service, I can understand that this was actually a sacrificial act of love on his part. My Mum on the other hand, would recount how she would have to close her eyes when watching me dance in a competition, as her mother's love couldn't bear to see anything go wrong for me! I see her mirror image in me to this day, as when I watch something like the English TV series, "Dancing On Ice," I find myself hiding my face behind a cushion, whenever a couple performs a dangerous move, in case there should be a fall or a mishap.

"I win," my older brother chimed. It was so annoying, he was always better than me at everything, and he always won every game we played. He was also one of those fortunate people who seem to have a natural intelligence. Oh I am not saying he didn't study, but he seemed to sail through exams with minimal effort. Whereas for me, every achievement and success came through hard graft and sheer grit – I think I missed the queue where natural intelligence was given out! However, I worked my way through the eleven+ to a place at the Grammar School.

Even the layout of the building was a challenge and called for higher intelligence! There were three blocks, A, B and C, with three floors each, so negotiating your timetable meant navigating from block to block and floor to floor. Confusion could sometimes lead to the cardinal sin of being late for a lesson. This was not as great a sin though as the length of your school skirt. It was the era of the mini skirt, and by rolling over your waistband, you could be fashionable even in your school uniform. Woe betide you though if you weren't quick enough to adjust it when you encountered the deputy headmistress. She would make you kneel down on the floor and she would use her ruler to measure the number of inches above the knee. If you were a transgressor, you would find yourself in detention.

Not that I ever found myself in that position, known as a "goody two shoes," always desperate to please and to be "good enough" in other people's estimation.

Choose life

Riding on an open top bus along Brighton seafront, blowing bubbles as we went, or dodging the waves as they broke over the promenade in Hove on a blustery day. At fifteen years old, the Wayfarers youth group had opened up a whole new social life for me, freeing me somewhat from the strict regimes of dancing and academic studies. However, that wasn't the only thing that opened up to me. As I observed and listened to the youth group leaders and some of the other members of the group, I felt that they were living in 3D, whereas I was living in 2D. As I questioned them, I discovered that there was a sense in which this was true.

They explained to me that they believed that God so wanted a personal relationship with each of us, that he had sent Jesus into our world to pay the price for all our wrong doings. Through a simple prayer, asking God for his forgiveness for doing things our own way, we could have a fresh start with Jesus in the driving seat. In the words of Psalm 37:5 TPT "Give God the right to direct your life, and as you trust him along the way, you'll find he pulled it off perfectly!" When they had taken that step, their spirit had come alive and in a true sense they had started living in 3D – alive in body, soul and spirit. There is a verse in the Old Testament where God encourages us to walk with him and in so doing to choose life (Deuteronomy 30:19). A colleague once told me that what he admired about me was the way I took life by the scruff of the neck and shook out of it everything I wanted. This desire for everything life offers made me want this relationship with God that I could see was making their lives richer.

A simple prayer, that was all they said it took, but I prayed it again and again, and nothing happened, I never felt any different. Being prone to an analytical mind, this was a real challenge. I pondered it over and over, perhaps I wasn't good enough for God either (that old mindset raises its head again)? Six difficult months followed, in which my Mum became seriously worried about my agonising over it all. I tried to determine what I was doing wrong – I didn't seem to have the strategies to make my way through this one.

Great times of fun and friendship, that's what weekends away with the youth group added up to, but this particular one also brought a turning point, with a wise lady's challenge. "What is it that you are struggling with, Sally, that is preventing you having this relationship with God?" She asked gently.

"Nothing happens when I say the prayer, so I must be doing something wrong, or perhaps I am just not good enough for God," I told her, close to tears.

She seemed to understand, and then she shared a verse in the Bible with me:

"Here I am! I stand at the door and knock. If anyone hears my voice and opens the door, I will come in and eat with that person, and they with me" (Revelation 3:20 NIV).

She explained that the verse said, "I will come in," not "I might," and not "I'll come in when you are good enough." The penny finally dropped, I could never be good enough of my own accord, the whole reason Jesus had to die on the cross was to make me acceptable to God. The wise lady also shared with me the analogy, that you can say you believe a chair will take your weight, but you don't prove your faith until you actually sit on it. So I finally took the step of faith and believed that on my invitation, Jesus did come into my life. There was no flash, bang, wallop, but a wonderful peace, and an inner awareness that my spirit had come alive and now I could begin to live in 3D. As the years go by, it is like a journey from outer space to earth, with all the bumps along the way. From a far off distance, the earth looks 2D, but as you travel closer, you realise it is 3D. Then as you hone in even further, you discover that the life on earth is also 3D. In the same way, the closer I walk with God, the more I experience of this 3D life.

Living with and for God is certainly not the easy option! If you want to live life to the full, you have to be willing to live on the edge. Over the years there have been doubts and failings on my part, but one thing I am convinced of, is that God is faithful. He often speaks to me through pictures, and one he gave me is that my name is written in the Book of Life in indelible ink, and nothing and no one (including me) can rub it out, for which I am eternally grateful.

Chapter 2

It Takes a Village to Raise a Child –
Meet Gibson

The runt of the litter

On January 23rd 1975, Esther was struggling to deliver her overdue baby. This drama was being played out in a small provincial hospital on the Island of Malaita in the Solomon Islands. She and Lionel already had four children, but their fifth, a little girl, had sadly died at birth. Would her sixth make it? He came out small and scrawny, fighting for his life, and they placed him in a bottle (an incubator in Western terms). But he pulled through, he was a survivor!

It may have been due to this difficult start, or due to the fact that he was the baby of the family, that his Mum always favoured him. Plus, with three older sisters and a tight-knit village community, there was always plenty of mothering. Some rivalry too, as his nearest sibling was his only brother, who was six years his senior, and next to their Dad, liked to be the boss of the family.

It was hard work in the garden, where Mum grew root crops, pineapple plants and fruit trees, to provide food for her family, and surplus to sell at the local market. Gibson's sisters would care for him when Mum went to the garden, sometimes taking him down to the side of the sea in the heat of the day so that he could feel the cool breeze. What excitement when Mum returned home bearing treats. Bananas, or a pineapple, or sweet rope (small yellow fruits) tied up in a banana leaf parcel. He would eagerly untie the tree bark string to reveal his treasure, then piercing the skins with his nail, he would suck up the sweet seeds inside.

As the years passed, the adventures increased. Gibson was allowed to follow the steep trail with his parents to climb up to the garden on the hillside. It was tiring for little legs, but it was worth it for what followed. Dad had built a small hut in the garden, and when there was a break in the work, Mum would cook some food over a small fire, and they would share stories and laugh together. Idyllic days that would pass all too soon.

The beating of the drum

"Naku lalakwa lae la sukulu, Naku lalakwa lae la sukulu!"[1] ("I don't want to go to school, I don't want to go to school!"). Why would you want to go to school when you have enjoyed being the centre of attention at home, the one taken on garden adventures, and on top of that, your Dad had bought you a new football? But school was a pathway to a better life in the Solomon Islands, and therefore you were sent on your way with more than gentle encouragement. When the drumbeat sounded to warn that school would soon start at 8am, Mum would drag Gibson along the road, pitching her greater strength against his. If he managed to escape her grip and beat a retreat, a coconut midrib would be swished at his heels to chivvy him along the way. However, as the bar was set, that football had to wait for after school, he settled in, and was proud to sit in his classroom on the wooden chair at the wooden desk that his Dad had made for him.

TGIF - "Thank God It's Friday" was the cry that went up every Friday in term time, because that afternoon was dedicated to sports. Bare-footed youngsters would show off their skills as budding footballers, and if by any chance there wasn't a football available, they would weave one out of coconut leaves. Even in the warm rain, the huge muddy puddles were not a deterrent to these young competitors. After the game, hot and sweaty from the tropical heat and their concerted efforts, they would go and jump into the big river, where there was much splashing, wrestling, ducking and diving.

---

[1] This is Gibson's language, Toabaita.

After school in the afternoons the younger kids would follow the example of the older kids, gathering down by the sea. They quickly learned to shimmy up the coconut palms to lob down fresh green coconuts, and breaking them open with a rock, they would feast on the soft white flesh inside. They progressed from spearing small fish in the shallow sea, to diving for fish around the coral reef, and in the process learning to swim would come naturally. Learning to balance a canoe was also an early skill learnt, after a few times of capsizing!

From father to son

Helping carry the dirty plates, pots and spoons to the bamboo water supply for washing up was a chore, but a chore that had to be done. But when Dad called you to work alongside him, well that was a different matter. "Come on Son, we have a project this holiday, we need to build a kitchen." Gibson would watch as his Dad cut different thicknesses and lengths of wood, and wove sago palm leaves into walling. As he took in how his Dad worked, he would be allowed to use the tools and join in the work, thus learning the cultural skills that had been passed down from generation to generation. Dad was also quick to acknowledge Gibson's contribution to the completed project, letting him share in the sense of achievement.

As an ex-navy man, Dad's grace and patience did not always hold strong. The young Gibson would accompany him on fishing trips, being given the responsibility of manoeuvring the canoe whilst Dad dived into the depths of the sea for clam shells. After holding his breath for what seemed an eternity, Dad would burst back above the water gasping as if his lungs would burst, and drop the precious clam shells into the canoe. But sometimes, Gibson would lose sight of his father beneath the surface, and the canoe would drift with the current. As Dad sought to resurface, he banged his head on the base of the canoe, and it was not complimentary words that came out of his mouth!

Reflecting on this in later years, Gibson would smile about this, as he too experienced this desperate need for air when deep sea diving – the benefit of hindsight for putting things into perspective.

A legacy of faith

It could have been a very different story, thought Esther, as she looked back on the early days of her marriage. The smoking, the drinking, the cursing, what a shock for this child bride, given in an arranged marriage at the tender age of fifteen, to a man twelve years her senior. To not agree to the marriage would be to dishonour tribal customs, and as was also the custom, she went to live with his family while he was away at sea. They were not unkind to her, but this home environment was a far cry from her parents' home, where they practised the Christian faith. However, hers was not a borrowed faith that had just been handed down by her parents, but a rich personal relationship with her Lord, Jesus Christ. So she stood firm, laboured in prayer, and was allowed to attend the local church.

Her husband was tolerant of her faith, but "it was not for him," not until the day he developed a large growth which confined him to bed. Then he presented her with a challenge, "Pray for me. If your God heals me, I will go to church with you."

This young woman of faith took up the gauntlet, confident in her God. She was inspired by the way God had worked in the Old Testament stories. Hadn't God used the young man David to slay the giant Goliath? Hadn't he shut the mouths of the lions when Daniel was thrown in their den for not agreeing to bow down and worship the king? She prayed, and the miracle happened! The growth shrunk and then completely disappeared. Her husband kept his word and accompanied her to church, and there the next miracle occurred, when he had an encounter with the living God and surrendered his life to his Lordship.

The young Gibson would sleep between his Dad and Mum, this man and woman of faith, on their homemade bed. He would often wake at 3am, hearing his Mum in fervent prayer, and his last memory of the night before would be his Dad sitting late into the night studying the scriptures by the light of the kerosene lamp. His Dad grew quickly in wisdom and godly counsel, and the couple were asked to pastor the local church. This meant that early night sleeps for Gibson were often spent on a mat on the church mud floor, whilst his Dad and Mum led meetings, and then he would be carried home over his Dad's shoulders.

"Pastor Ben, Pastor Ben" the children would call out as Gibson's Dad visited their homes. Gibson's Dad was a shepherd in the true sense of the word. He would visit the people of the community, listening to them and praying for them, showing a deep sense of love and care. Looking down from heaven today, he would be proud to see these qualities in his son.

Listening in at evening time at one of the houses built on stilts in the small village of Onebusu, you would be enchanted to hear the harmonious melodies rising and falling within. The self-taught Gibson would be accompanying the family on his ukulele or guitar, as they sang old hymns and choruses. He had known Jesus from when he was knee high to a grasshopper, and he loved to worship, but salvation comes through a personal decision to follow Jesus. So it was that he was sitting in a meeting when someone sang out these words:

"I heard a preacher say in John 3:16
God so loved the world that he gave us his only Son
I was sitting at the back and listening as he preached
And a voice came within me, Jesus loves you too

I gave my life that day for the One who makes me sing
All my cares and burdens were completely gone
A new road to walk and a new step to take
Now I'll walk with you through all eternity."

Gibson felt propelled off his seat to go and kneel at the altar and give his life to Jesus, and that commitment has not wavered till today. Yes, there was some roguish behaviour, and scars to show from misadventures, but his faith penetrated his core like a steel rod in his backbone.

Chapter 3

Spreading My Wings

Sally flies the nest

"Go as far away from home as possible." This was my older brother's advice when I was applying to go to teacher training college – he obviously thought it was time I flew the nest. So I found myself on a National Express Coach from London to Bradford to attend an interview. When we stopped at the service station at Leicester Forest, I already felt I was in a foreign land – I asked a server how the drinks machine worked and I didn't understand a word of her reply! When later I secured a place at the college, a southerner acquaintance who was studying there sent me a Yorkshire English dictionary to ease my transition. And "Eeh by gum" (oh my god) it was cold up there.

If I gritted my teeth hard enough, I was sure I could stop the tears from running down my cheeks, as the train sped north and I watched my Mum's figure recede on Kings Cross Station. This was really it, I was on my own, yet I now knew the One who has promised to be with us always (Matthew 28:20). But this new independence brought many challenges: from college meals (I had always been a fussy eater), to shrinking the hand-knitted jumper my Mum made me by putting it in too hot a wash; from trying the disco scene to fit in, to trying to drown out the erotic noises coming from a neighbouring bedroom; from making cups of coffee for policemen, whom we thought were whiling away their time, only to discover the wife of the Yorkshire Ripper was at our college, to struggling with doubts about my faith, yet realising that life without God in it now would be no life at all.

Working life

Letter after letter received no response even though I cast my net far and wide. There was a shortage of teaching jobs in England in the late 1970s. Then, as they say, at the eleventh hour, I landed a job, right there in Bradford – it seemed it was to be my home, and I was to become a converted northerner, not that I have ever mastered the Bradford accent!

Selfishly, my favourite class to teach was the Reception class, the children just starting school, as I could then mould them before any other teacher got their hands on them (metaphorically speaking of course!). There was no time to think about anything else from the moment the children entered the room to the moment they left. And it was a complete myth buster that teachers have an easy life with long holidays – I worked long, hard hours, and my friends were roped into preparing practical materials on social nights out!

Every child was special to me, and perhaps it was this ethos that helped me up the promotion ladder. "What would you do if you had a very difficult morning in the classroom?" was a question fired at me during an interview for a more senior post at a multicultural school. I can't remember my answer, but I vividly remember a fellow interviewee telling me that she had answered that she would go and get drunk at lunchtime. Perhaps it was no surprise that I was offered the job over her, but having accepted the post, I later gave back word, as a more exciting opportunity opened up.

"What a loss to the teaching profession," this was one of the greatest compliments ever made to me, by a deputy head and former colleague, when she heard that I had agreed to take up a post with a group of churches writing teaching materials and training volunteers. It had some kudos being asked to work in a full time role alongside an all male church staff, and there were many achievements to celebrate. However, it also led to some very dark days in my life. Volunteers I trained seemingly perceived me as confident and self-assured, but that "not good enough" tag hadn't died within me, especially in a male dominated environment. Add to this the fact that I was working in a basement office with no outside light, and gradually I sunk into a depression. I battled with dark thoughts, and eventually I was asked to leave the post as I was struggling so much that I was not perceived as being a people's person.

Where was God in this, you may ask? Well, actually, he was right in the centre of it. King David wrote in the Psalms, "Even though I walk through the darkest valley, I will fear no evil, for you are with me, your rod and your staff, they comfort me." (Psalm 23) But there was also a vital lesson for me to learn, a lesson about the battle for the mind, that is a battle most of us fight. This whole experience started me on my lifelong journey of taking every thought captive and subjecting it to Christ (2 Corinthians 10:5), learning to think on whatever is true, noble, right, pure, lovely, admirable, excellent and praiseworthy (Philippians 4:9). I recommend this as the Three Rs - Recognise whether a thought meets these criteria; if it doesn't Reject it; and possibly most important of all, Replace it with a thought that does meet the criteria. It is a lesson that has served me well for the rest of my life.

"A bruised reed he will not break, and a smouldering wick he will not snuff out, till he has brought justice through to victory." (Matthew 12:20) These were words written about Jesus, and I certainly felt like a 'bruised reed' after losing my job, but as always, my God proved faithful. I did some supply teaching, but incredibly I was successful in my application for a primary advisory teacher post, which was a promotion from when I left teaching. Following this I moved onto a deputy headship, and it was here I witnessed the truth of the words of Henry Adams: "A teacher affects eternity; he can never tell where his influence stops." One of the boys I taught, I met later in my life, and he was in a key leadership role in a charity I worked for.

I never thought of myself as a career girl, but that seemed to be the way life led me. The joy of being the headteacher of a small Church of England First School, which was like being the head of a large family made up of eight adults and 120 children. But as time went on, it was too parochial, and I wanted to branch out further. So the privilege followed of setting up a Children's Services Unit in a Local Authority, which sadly shortly after my appointment, failed its OFSTED inspection and went through the turbulent time of the ousting of the Chief Education Officer (CEO). You can imagine the stresses of that job, but ironically, as the CEO left, he told me that he admired my work, and that I had proved wrong his misgivings of appointing a spinster, and more than that, a spinster who professed her faith! Prejudice was still ripe in the mid 1990s.

The travel bug

Life was not all work and no play.

"What are your desires?" my friend Sarah asked me as we walked along the beach with the breeze in our hair and the sand between our toes. "I want to travel the world," I replied with enthusiasm.

"Then you will," she continued, "I believe God doesn't only fulfil our desires when we delight in him, but he puts those desires in our hearts in the first place" (Psalm 37:4). How right she was, and what a mighty God I serve, having now visited six of the seven continents of our world – only Antartica left to go!

Eye openers came in the form of a trip to a Romanian orphanage caring for children after the fall of Nicolas Ceausescu's communist regime, and another trip with a group of teachers to Kazakhstan to share our education expertise, where as honoured guests we were served with the Kazak delicacy of a sheep's head – I can't remember how we managed to pass it politely around the table without partaking. Holiday adventures: riding camels on the beach in Kenya on Christmas Day; night swimming in the sea in

Cha-am, Thailand; a picnic meal at Sydney Harbour to watch the New Year's Eve fireworks; and too many others to recount here.

Africa changes you forever

"Africa changes you forever, like nowhere on earth. Once you have been there, you will never be the same." – Brian Jackman.

Having been the first woman to be given the opportunity to preach at church, many more opportunities had followed, and unbeknown to me, overseas visitors had listened in. So to my delight, I received an invitation to go and preach in Zambia. Roma and Catherine led a number of churches in different areas of the country and they had planned a series of meetings, from the capital Lusaka, to Ndola and Kitwe, and to the border with the Congo in the north. I was really concerned how the person meeting me at the provincial airport would recognise me, in my naivety not realising that I would be the only white woman emerging from the plane.

My most memorable experience was going to take meetings at a camp in the bush. As we drove into a clearing in dense woods, ladies emerged from all directions, singing songs of welcome and waving branches. It was my idea of heaven. The camp was very basic by western terms, but an incredible achievement: accommodation huts for about 600 ladies of all ages; pit latrines within straw enclosures; daily provision of meals; and hundreds of ladies sitting on the grass drinking in the word of God. Another strong memory is when I had to drive a lady to the nearest hospital, as I was the only driver on site and the lady was going into labour!

At the northern border with the Congo, we stayed at a clinic run by a white Christian lady, who had been there for many years. Another desire I had was to see the birth of a baby, and a lovely African lady allowed me to be in attendance for the birth of her sixth child. I have to say, that probably due to it being her sixth child, the baby just popped out without any moaning or groaning on the mother's part.

It was a most moving experience, and as I cradled the newborn in my arms, there were tears of wonder in my eyes.

Can't you go any further away?

Sitting on the rocks in Turkey, looking out over the sea, was an ideal place to talk and listen to God. It was here that I knew God was telling me it was time to go and work abroad. On returning home to England, I talked to my church Pastor, and then I started looking into what possibilities there were. I looked into missionary work, but most openings were linked to distinct denominations, then I applied to Voluntary Service Overseas (VSO). The recruitment process included questions as to whether you preferred a hot or cold climate, a no-brainer in my case, as Africa had a place in my heart. Due to my education experience, I was given more than one option of placement, and one option was the Solomon Islands, to which my response was, "Where are the Solomon Islands?" I was sent down to the basement at the VSO headquarters in London to look at a world map and I discovered that these tiny islands were in the Pacific Ocean, northeast of Australia.

It did not take long for me to accept the placement. Being an in-service teacher trainer, in an island paradise of sandy beaches and coconut palms, sounded like a dream. It was my Mum, who always supported me in everything I did, that asked the question "Can't you go any further away?" However, a lot more water went under the bridge before my eventual departure. I failed my medical and had to have an operation before I was given fitness clearance; then the planned posting in July 1999 was delayed due to political unrest in the Solomon Islands. So it was, that in September 1999, I found myself boarding a plane with other volunteers that I didn't know, to travel to the other side of the world, with a mixture of excitement and trepidation.

Chapter 4

Gibson – Home and Away

Survival of the fittest

Hungry, hungry, always hungry, the cry of the boys' dormitory at Adaua High School, where Gibson attended after his primary school years. Of course they were provided with meals, but there was never enough for growing teenagers. The hunger pains even made the two hours' walk home some weekends worth it to eat home kaikai (food), even though it meant another two hours' walk back again on Sunday afternoon, but you had been refuelled by then. And what treasure when Gibson's sister gave him the money to buy a tin of tuna at the school canteen, a tin of tuna all to himself, after what felt like a lifetime of sharing one tin among many in the village.

Hidden under his bed was a small pot and a 10kg bag of rice. When he was overcome with stomach rumblings, he would sneak off into the bush, make a small fire and cook himself a snack. But as the term progressed, he was surprised to see the rice disappearing from his bag quicker than his cooking schedule. The mystery was solved when one of his friends was sick and excused from gardening duties. Staying behind in the dormitory, pretending to sleep, he spied on the older boys, who made a small hole in the rice bag and through a straw, siphoned some of the rice off into their own pots. You didn't challenge them, they ruled the roost. But, as Gibson found out, there were limits to how far the 'ringleaders' could go. In a later memory he recalls their 'day of judgement.'

"Come out and join us!"

Waving banners and shouting, the older boys mustered the younger ones to join their protest. They were rebelling against the discipline of the principal, and it was more than the younger boys' lives were worth not to join in. There was status in seniority. Gibson recounts a strange mixture of fear and excitement, as they marched behind the ring leaders, waving their banners "Demote the Principal." It was a long trek to Malu'u town, where the education office was situated, and the principal arrived by truck ahead of them. The education officer came out to pacify the main protagonists, but in time they got their comeuppance, as they were expelled! Gibson, as a conscript, was of course spared this fate, but he had experienced a spark of the passion that would burn within him and spur him on in the future.

Gibson moving on

"The school truck is coming, the school truck is coming," excited shouts as the truck came back from the town of Auki, bringing messages, letters and treats from families. Boarding school students would wait in anticipation to see if something had their name on it. Indeed there was a message for Gibson, but not one he wanted to see. It read, "Dad is very sick with pneumonia and has been admitted to the main hospital." What a blow in the midst of his studies. He struggled through to the end of the school year, took his exams in a fog of confusion, and then returned home. The strong bond he had with his Dad grew even stronger when Dad came home from hospital. Gibson helped his Mum to nurse his Dad through the last weeks of his life, a heavy burden for a young man, but there were some special moments sharing heart to heart.

His Dad wanted his legacy of faith to live on in this son. "Son, always remember to keep your focus on the Lord. He is the vine, we are the branches, when we remain in him we will bear much fruit (John 15:5). Look to him and He will give you success in every area of your life." On another occasion his Dad addressed matters of the heart. "Please take care of your Mum when I go ahead of her to glory, and soon son, it will be time to take a wife of your own. Don't focus your choice on outward beauty alone, character is much more important, that is what will stand the test of the years." These words were part of the shaping and moulding of Gibson's life, but they didn't in any way diminish the great sense of loss when in February 1995 his Dad took his last breath. Dad was at peace knowing he was going to see his Lord and Saviour, but it is always harder for those who are left behind, and for Gibson it left a big gap in his life.

With Dad gone, there was no money for Gibson to complete his education. This gave rise to a huge sense of disappointment, and the questions that many of us ask, even those of us who put our trust in God, "Why me, Lord? My sister is a trained teacher, and my brother is training to be a teacher, what future is there for me?" It seemed the end of the road in many senses, but the fighter in him rose up again. His story is reminiscent of the English folklore of Dick Whittington, who packed his bag and set off for London to find his fortune. Gibson's brother was returning to teacher training college in the capital Honiara, on the Island of Guadalcanal. Gibson packed his bag and set off with him, into an unknown future, heart in mouth, but trusting his Dad's words, that as he looked to the Lord, the Lord would give him success.

Honiara was a shock to his system, like being thrust into the big wide world. Arriving at the wharf in the passenger vessel, he marvelled at the huge container ships. Disembarking, he was apprehensive of the cars and taxis that seemed to fly in all directions, and felt he took his life in his hands to cross the roads. The people passing by him shoulder to shoulder were no longer extended family or tribal neighbours. The shops displayed a huge variety of goods, including treasures from the West such as tape cassette players. All in all, his senses were overwhelmed by these new experiences and the general cacophony of activity.

A message had been sent ahead to Gibson's uncle, who was a policeman. "Now that your brother has passed on, his son, Gibson, is coming to Honiara to look for work. Please honour your late brother by taking this son into your home and your family." Apprehension filled Gibson's heart. Would he be accepted by the family? Would he be able to break out of the narrow mindset of village life? Would he be able to find work?

The dream

A newspaper advert brought the first breakthrough.

"SEA KING - NEW CHINESE RESTAURANT OPENING - WAITING STAFF REQUIRED"

Despite his lack of experience, Gibson was thrilled to be successful in his application, along with fourteen other young men and women. The business was owned and run by a family from Taiwan, who treated these young employees as family, training them, and winning their hearts by feeding them well! Gibson was enjoying working at the restaurant and hadn't been there long, when a well-built, smartly dressed Islander came into the restaurant one lunchtime and sat at one of the tables Gibson was serving.

Gibson: "May I take your order Sir?"

It was as the gentleman replied, that Gibson realised he wasn't speaking in Solomon Island's Pidjin (a broken English).

Gentleman: "Yes you may, I'll have sweet and sour pork please. But let me introduce myself. My name is Robert, and I am a Pastor of a church in Vanuatu. I have come here to tell you that I saw you in a dream, and my church wants to pay for you to come to a conference in my country of Vanuatu."

Gibson: "You must be wrong Sir. It can't be me, there are lots of waiters in restaurants in Honiara."

Gentleman: "No son, it was definitely you I saw in my dream."

Gibson was shocked, and in disbelief, but on finishing his meal, the gentleman went and spoke to the boss to ask permission for Gibson to go. All Gibson's colleagues were agog, and were pleading with Gibson to ask for them to go as well! The boss was amazed and delighted, proud that one of his customers should make such an offer, and proud, believing it must have been down to the good service that his employee had provided. As Robert left the restaurant, he promised, "I will be back in touch."

Nothing happened for a long time, and as the year progressed, Gibson carried on his day to day work and wondered if this extraordinary meeting itself had been a dream. However, in July, four months after their encounter, the gentleman, Robert, rang the restaurant to speak to Gibson and tell him that he was sending his air ticket to attend the conference in October. It was not easy to convince others though that this adventure would actually come about. Gibson had to persuade his brother to interrupt his teacher training studies, to help him apply for his first ever passport. Then, in September, Gibson went to the Solomon Airlines office to collect his ticket. The lady was somewhat suspicious, it seemed just as incredible to her as it was to Gibson himself, that a gentleman he had only met once, had bought him a ticket to fly to Vanuatu, but the ticket itself was evidence enough.

God makes a way

This village boy had never been to the airport, or seen a plane close up. His big brother, now fully persuaded, accompanied him to the airport and stood by him as he checked in. Then he dropped the bombshell, "This is as far as I can come Gibson, you have to go through on your own."

Gibson nearly choked on his reply, "But you can't leave me here, I don't know what to do."

"Sorry, small bro, only those who are flying are allowed to go beyond this point."

With butterflies rampant in his stomach, he walked through the barrier, straining for a last glimpse of his brother's face, until it was finally blocked out of sight. But God made a way. A young man from Vanuatu who was studying in Honiara was on the same flight, and he guided him through the boarding process. Once he was strapped into his seat, Gibson's relief, mixed with awe at the goodness of God in making this opportunity possible for him, overflowed in unashamed tears flowing down his face.

As the plane took off, it was the most incredible experience. He felt like he was floating alone in the sky and he recalled the scripture in Isaiah 40:31, "Those who hope in the Lord will renew their strength. They will soar on wings like eagles; they will run and not grow weary, they will walk and not be faint." However, the two-hour flight was over all too quickly for Gibson, and as the announcement was made to fasten seat belts ready for landing, he again felt a sense of trepidation, what awaited him at Port Vila Airport, Vanuatu?

As he came down the steps of the plane, his eyes were automatically drawn to the viewing platform. New waves of emotion hit him, as he saw Pastor Robert with all his family, smiling broadly and waving down at him. Inside the arrivals hall, there was a welcome party of senior men from the church. A flower garland was placed around his neck and he was treated like a dignitary. He was overwhelmed, he was a village boy, the youngest in his family, but again he recalled words from the Bible, "The Lord does not look at the things man looks at. Man looks at the outward appearance, but the Lord looks at the heart." (1 Samuel 16:7) There were still further shocks to come, when at the opening of the conference he was greeted with a kiss on each cheek (Vanuatu was previously a French colony), a totally foreign tradition to Gibson. At the end of that first, heady day, all his emotions culminated in laughter and tears, as he was shown to his room, the first time in his life that he had a bedroom all to himself.

The conference passed in wave upon wave of wonder – playing in the band; a first opportunity to play an electric guitar; and introducing himself as the sole representative of the Solomon Islands. He obviously made an impression too, as the following year, he was invited back, and sent a ticket again!

The sacrifice

Life was moving along swimmingly for Gibson in Honiara. He had moved on from the Sea King restaurant and found other employment in the Honiara Hotel, and then the Yacht Club. These venues were frequented by tourists, business people and politicians, many of them expats. This is where Gibson gained confidence in practising the English he had learnt at school – an important development for his future, although he did not know it at the time! However, it was as he was honing his skills that his working life was interrupted by another message that came from his Mum at home. "Please come home son, I need your help." With a somewhat heavy heart, but a strong sense of duty, and his Dad's words still ringing in his ears, Gibson made plans and returned to his home Island of Malaita. He had become used to having some money in his pocket, but opportunities for earning were few and far between at home. His Mum needed his financial support, but she also wanted him to continue his Dad's legacy of serving in the church.

There was nothing else for it, the only work to be had was harvesting coconuts for copra – hard, manual work that built muscles where you didn't know you had muscles. Once the coconuts were gathered, you split them open and used a copra knife to scape out the flesh. This was packed hard into copra sacks and carried to the drier – shouldering the sacks made Gibson sympathise with beasts of burden. The next part of the process was just as excruciating. The coconut flesh was loaded into old oil drums and dried above the intense heat of burning logs and coconut husks. As the sweat ran off you in the tropical heat, it was as if every drop of sweat earned you another cent. However, it was all worthwhile when weighed against his Mum's gratitude, and running alongside this hard labour, he had become the Youth Pastor of the church and was finding great fulfilment in mentoring others in the faith. He would lead them in mission trips to other churches on the Island, where they would perform dramas and action songs.

Sacrifice never goes unnoticed by God. Gibson's uncle, Father Richard, was a priest in the Anglican Church, and he was one of those who had invited Gibson to bring the youth to perform in his church. He had been watching Gibson's life, and in 1998, he went to visit Gibson in his village.

"Son, for the last couple of years I have been to Australia through the Southern Cross Institute for a global prayer conference. This year, due to other commitments, I am unable to go, and I would like you to go in my place – all your expenses will be paid."

Gibson could scarcely take it in, another overseas trip with all expenses paid? But sure enough, he found himself flying off to Brisbane with three older men who were all leaders in their churches. They made a two-day road trip to Canberra, where they attended the conference meetings. There were other experiences which, unbeknown to Gibson, would be signposts into his future. They met Steve Grace, an Australian Christian singer, who took them to visit his recording studio, and they had the honour of being allowed to go into Government House in Canberra to pray for the Australian parliament.

The future lay wide open before Gibson, his future travelling would take him to places he had never even dreamed of.

Chapter 5

The Other Side Of The World

So, Voluntary Service Overseas (VSO) sent me to the other side of the world, and the whole experience of living in the Solomon Islands was amazing. Thus, I am going to dedicate this chapter to newsletters that I wrote whilst I was there. The friends who printed and distributed the newsletters for me back in England gave them the title:

Salutations

NUIS LONG SOLOMON AELANS

(Solomon Islands Pijin English for News from the Solomon Islands)

September 1999

If you could see me now...

Imagine the scene from a Robinson Crusoe film – long sandy beaches bordered by coconut palms, clear blue sea and clear blue skies. This was the picture that greeted us as we approached the coast of Isabel (an island province) in our motorised canoe. We started on a forty-minute walk through the bush to reach the village of Salio, where we were going to stay for the next five days to learn Pidgin English.

The seven of us volunteers were given a custom leaf house to stay in – these houses are built on stilts, have large window frames and low sloping roofs, so they are cool and dark inside. A special pit latrine toilet had been built for the visitors some distance from the house. Washing of self (wrapped in a lava lava cloth) and clothes were done under the standpipe or in a beautiful pool in the nearby river. The rising drum sounded any time from 4.20 am, and although we tried to please by attending morning service, when we arrived at the church at 7.00 am we had already missed the first half hour! The incense swinging and the white robes seemed a little incongruous compared to the bare-footed congregation and wild pigs running around outside.

Evenings were spent storytelling by the light of kerosene lamps, or we were delighted by a visit from the children, who entertained us with harmony singing. All the villagers treated us like royalty and our farewell party on the last evening was the best night out I had had in a long time, complete with bamboo band and very lively dancing.

Back at base in Honiara, we have been undergoing a fairly rigorous induction programme which, along with adjusting to lifestyle, climate, and each other, has left us exhausted. This last couple of days the teacher trainers amongst us have been introduced to the Primary Education Development Project, which seems to be of excellent quality. We have met our Solomon Islander counterparts and we are getting geared up to move on to our bases in the provinces. This must be one of the most beautiful countries on the face of God's earth – what more can I say than "Wish you were" and make sure some of you start making plans to come and visit me.

December 1999

Happy Christmas and a very happy Millennium!

About ten weeks have passed since my first newsletter, and I feel as if I have lived another entire lifetime. In some ways this is a very solitary world, where thoughts and emotions are shared only between God and I, and my diary. In other ways, I sometimes crave for my own space, as it seems like living in Piccadilly Circus in the rush hour. Nothing is the same as England, so it is hard to give you points of reference, yet coming back to Honiara, Guadalcanal this week, has reinforced the fact that Auki, (main town in Malaita province) is now home. So, here are some of the highs and lows of my first term …

Accommodation – I have a lovely, spacious wooden house in Auki, at the top of a steep hill – walking is the predominant means of getting around, so I am getting fit. The house has a wonderful balcony, which catches cool breezes and gives a splendid view down over the sea by day and displays glorious sunsets by night. The new moon is upside down here, and some stars twinkle with the colours of the rainbow. Two other volunteers share the house, Rita and Steve – Rita (who came out the same time as me) is another primary teacher trainer and Steve works for the Malaitan Sports Council. Steve is away a lot, but was used to allowing anyone and everyone to stay at the house, hence the comparison with Piccadilly Circus in the rush hour! This has become more of a challenge when there has been no water in the house for several days and water must be carried to the house in buckets, or when you get up in the morning to find that someone has used up all the made-up powdered milk or juice yet again!

Pests – In the first few weeks I was sleeping in a downstairs room, as someone had the key to my upstairs bedroom and we couldn't get into that room. During this time, we had rats, and although we successfully caught one in a trap, I could hear them in the night. Then one evening, a visitor spotted a rat entering by the Louvre windows, so we closed the windows hoping to stem the invasion. It did, but the same night we were burgled whilst we were in bed and a two-legged rat walked off with my short-wave radio and the chocolate in the fridge (a present from the visitor from Honiara). Things have calmed down a little in the house, although last Saturday I looked out of the window at the sound of a falling tree and shouted at Rita to move, as she was filling a bucket at the standpipe in the garden. A neighbour had decided to cut down a tree because it looked dangerous, but it had fallen the wrong way, narrowly missing Rita and cutting off our power supply. I rushed out and bought another kerosene lamp, but power had been restored by evening.

Volunteers – There are about fifteen volunteers now based in Auki, ranging in age from late twenties to early sixties, but the majority act like overgrown students. There have been some good trips out to the beach and a couple of lovely evenings with bamboo bands, but their main form of entertainment is Solbrew, the local beer.

Work – I am fast forming the opinion that Solbrew is the curse of the nation. I have had an interesting term in my base school, where frustrations included teacher absences due to overindulgence in Solbrew the afternoon/evening before. At the beginning of term, I went into broken down, bare classrooms, but by the end of term the school had been transformed into a bright interesting learning environment. In Week 8, we held a workshop for 48 teachers, which went very well, and in Week 9 I was given a farewell send off, when children did custom dancing, and the teacher representative gave a farewell speech:

"The guest of honour, Miss Sally Husbegh (maiden name Hudspeth), on behalf of the Headteacher, his deputy and the staff of this school. It is a pleasure to take this opportunity to share with you our sympathy of heart. Sally, I must assure you that at the beginning of the moment you shared with us, I for one was one of those who bears in mind that you are wasting much of our time. Nevertheless, at the end of our wasted times we have come to understand that we have taken wrong ideas. Sally – we have believed that even though your visical being will not be with us, your very good ideas and experiences have grown like planted crops in our minds. Without taking much of your time on behalf of our team at this school, I would like to give you a very very big thanks."

Church – God definitely knew where he was putting me – the only Assemblies of God (AOG) Bible College in the Solomon Islands is based about a forty-five minute walk from my house, and the odd evening sessions I have been able to attend have been excellent. I am also attending the local AOG Church, but I still do not feel part of them. It is hard to get to know people. I did have one wonderful weekend in the North of the Island, at a village called Onoima, where I played with the pikininis in the sea and spoke at the AOG church on the Saturday evening, Sunday morning and Sunday evening. The Pastor there is a lovely lady called Jenny (twenty-six years old).

In conclusion – Am I pleased I came…? YES. What have I learnt…? How to speak Pidgin, how to weave a mat, how to hiss to stop a bus, how to bake without weighing scales, a lot about myself and other people, and that God is faithful all the time! What have I enjoyed…? Sunshine, swimming, snorkelling, fresh pineapple, bush lime (a drink made of squeezed limes), work achievements, letters and parcels from home. What can you pray for…? A good friend (or even a man in my life!), and more opportunities to share the Life and Word of God that's within me.

April 2000

What a long time ago December '99 and my last newsletter seem to be

It is this strange phenomenon of so much happening, but time passing so quickly. For those of you who haven't heard from me personally, I will try to continue the tale from where I left off last time…

Holiday in Western Province – Rita and I flew from Honiara to Western Province, where we had booked six nights between two eco-tourist lodges. The first was Matikuri and the second Vanua Rapita. At Matikuri we were the only guests, so when the owner and his wife went off visiting or shopping, we were alone on our desert island! The second lodge was even more beautiful than the first. Our leaf house had a large open sitting area, where you could watch the most amazing sunsets in panoramic splendour. We rode in canoes, spotted dolphins, and went to a local village celebration where we joined in with the island dancing.

Christmas – We returned to Auki for about five days before we set off to East Malaita to spend Christmas with the family of the head teacher of Rita's base school for Term

1, 2000. We had a room between us in the family leaf house, with a mattress each on the floor and each of us marked out our space by the erection of the all-important mosquito net. There was a leaf hut about 100 yards from the house with a bucket flush toilet and a pipe shower – very posh for the bush! Christmas Eve was the high spot of the stay for us – we visited Leilei Island, an uninhabited island a canoe ride away, where we swam in the clear, warm sea and drank coconut milk from the coconuts the boys shinned up the trees to get for us. Then in the evening back in the village, the panpipe band came to play for us and we danced the night away. Christmas Day was quiet – they do not exchange presents in the Solomon Islands, but we had taken some small gifts for the children. Christmas dinner was a bowl of rice with cucumber, banana and pineapple chopped in it!

Term 1, 2000 – My base school this term was Kakara Primary School, a village about forty-five minutes north of Auki by road. The first week I tried travelling back and forth each day, but transport was a problem, so from Week 2 I stayed in the village from Monday to Friday most weeks and I thoroughly enjoyed it. A couple from the Auki church let me use their house in the village and a lady called Margaret acted as house girl (a helper) for me, cooking my evening meal. The village was so peaceful and life is so simple – no electricity, so evenings saw me on the balcony telling stories or singing with the local pikininis by the light of a kerosene lamp. It was about a fifteen-minute walk down to the sea, so sometimes I was able to go for a swim after school. The school staff worked very hard, and as in my first term, the school underwent a total transformation during my stay. Parents were very appreciative and by the end of term, my morning walk to school was punctuated by cries of "Mone Sally" (Morning Sally), and I was really sad to leave them all.

Back at base in Auki – life could never be considered boring; there has been a catalogue of events. In January, we had four visits from a young man indecently exposing himself in the garden. In February, I had my purse stolen from my basket whilst I was in a store. Somebody caught the boy who was the culprit and the purse was returned fully intact, but I ended up in tears at the police station, when seven policemen started poking and hitting the boy. Also in February, Peggy, another VSO volunteer, came up to the house to receive a telephone call one night and whilst she was there, somebody came into the house and stole three pairs of shoes and an umbrella. In March, someone cut the pipe and made off with our gas bottle, then we had another break-in (through the only window left without security wire), and just before we came away to Honiara, Rita had a "creeping" incident (a man making advances outside the window). So.... VSO (Voluntary Service Overseas) have said they will pay for a security guard for us, we just have to find one!

What else is new? In January we were shocked to hear our project boss had been given another job in Jamaica and was leaving the Solomon Islands in February. The temporary contract of the in-service trainer also finished, so there are two jobs currently being advertised and I am putting in an application! In February, I was given the form to complete to apply to be licensed to preach in the Assemblies of God churches in the Solomon Islands. I wait for my first preaching date in the local church in Auki. My friend Clare plans to visit in June, the first friend to share my adventure here. So, plenty of items for prayer, and watch this space for the next exciting instalment!

Tuesday 6 June 2000

Newsflash 8pm – Rita and I are sitting on our balcony, eating chocolate crunch pudding (thanks to a parcel from England), and listening to the latest SIBC (Solomon Islands Broadcasting) news bulletin. The British Foreign Minister has announced that there is a coup in the Solomon Islands – Qantas has suspended all international flights due to security fears – telecommunications within and out from the country are severely restricted. And we are safe and well.

Bizarre is how I would describe the events of the last few days. We have had no telephone/fax/computer lines out of Auki for over two weeks now, which has been rather frustrating. Then on Monday, when I went down to the office, startling news started filtering through. The prime minister was being held under house arrest and Honiara/Guadacanal was under the control of the Malaitan Eagles (a militant group from Malaita Province) in conjunction with the police. This appears to have little effect on daily life in Malaita, except that many of us withdrew money from the banks in case cash supplies dried up.

"Great is thy faithfulness, O God my Father" are the words of one of my favourite hymns, and something God has proved to me time and time again. Today, as the man at Telekom tried for the sixth time to connect my call to England on the one available satellite phone, I prayed fervently, asking God for a miracle – the answer, two precious minutes talking to my friend Clare. Sadly, she confirmed that the British Government advice is not to travel to the Solomon Islands due to the political situation.

The work scene – my school this term has been harder work, yet the open day for the parents last week was truly rewarding. The children presented dramas, songs and custom dances, and teachers testified to the fruit of my labours. Another workshop, this time for 64 teachers, and a farewell song for Grace, my Solomon Islands counterpart, and I:

"Happy golden memories fly like the sparks of lightning
flash,
Memories of the past we'll treasure most
Like the rainbow in the sky your presence disappears,
Gone, gone forever-happy days
MEN: *Dear Sally and Grace thank you for teaching us*
WOMEN: *Dear Sally and Grace we will remember you*

May God bless you as you travel to Auki,
We will remember forevermore."

I didn't get shortlisted for the jobs, but towards the end of this term I was offered a transfer of placement by VSO to the teacher training college in Honiara, with an automatic extension to my VSO contract. Now of course, that is all on hold – if the situation does not get sorted out, VSO may withdraw from the Solomon Islands.

Food for thought – when I first became a Christian at fifteen years old, I was part of a youth group called "The Wayfarers" and we used to sing a song:

"I know who holds the future and he'll guide me with his hand
With God things don't just happen, everything by him is planned
So as I face tomorrow with its problems large and small
I'll trust the God of miracles, give to him my all."

I have been reminded of this song recently and I am very sure that I want to continue to give my all to my God of miracles.

Update – I am now in Ferring (West Sussex) with my parents – we were evacuated from Auki on Sunday 11 June. I spent four nights in Australia with Rita, and we arrived in London on Saturday 17 June.

Sally's Mum with the iconic beauty of her era

Sally's Dad debonair in his army uniform

Chapter 6

Searching For Love

Sally's heartache

"Go on, I dare you," my friend whispered in my ear as the gorgeous, blonde, thirteen year old boy in our form came around the corner. In my young eyes he looked like a Greek God, and the name his parents gave him seemed to confirm this – Magnus Magnusson! I tried to look nonchalant as I approached him (all the time wondering why I, of all people, was doing the asking), and I think I managed to get the words out fairly calmly, "We wondered if you'd like to come swimming with a couple of us?" He declined!

This set the tone for my romantic involvement, which followed me right into my forties. I always picked friends who were more attractive than me and more appealing to the opposite sex. Added to this, photos of my Mum and Dad in their younger years, showed my Mum with an iconic beauty of her era, and my Dad as debonair, especially in his army uniform – I would look in the mirror and think, "What happened to me?" My Mum commented what lovely legs I had, and I thought, yes I would be OK if I could walk round with a bag over my head! I hadn't grasped the concept that God says that He knits us together in our mothers' wombs and that we are fearfully and wonderfully made (Psalm 139:13-14). Perhaps I can be forgiven, as most of us struggle with our appearance in some way, particularly in our developing years – I am too short, too tall, too fat, too thin, and many other foolhardy comparisons.

There were some romantic forays over the years – I can remember the first kiss at thirteen, we were playing a game of spin the plate and the forfeit for not catching the plate was to kiss a boy! It was only a swift kiss on the lips, but it was full of public embarrassment for me as the uninitiated, and my mind played with the thought, "I bet he wishes it was someone else who didn't catch the plate." There was the male friend who was at college in Bath, which is a beautiful city in the Southwest of England. He invited me to go down for the weekend and his landlady kindly made us curry for lunch, my first time to taste the dish, and it took some swallowing for my conservative tastes. But the boys, and then men, that I liked, did not reciprocate my feelings, and the few who showed an interest in me, were not what I was looking for. Was I aiming too high?

The years passed and the heartache grew, as I watched my friends have boyfriends; get married; and have children, whilst I was still walking the single path. I knew I had so much love to give, but I could not believe anyone would love me enough to want to marry me, perhaps the shadow of "Not good enough" still following me. But in time, I learnt to embrace singleness, and believe that God had the best plan for my life. Looking back, I appreciate all the opportunities being single offered me, especially the freedom and finance to travel the world.

"Sticks and stones will break my bones, but words will never harm me"

"You're too fussy!" These words hit me like a poisonous arrow, shot by both Christians and non-Christians on different occasions. Surely my God of abundant love didn't want me to settle for second best?

Over the years, which seemed to stretch out for me, there were a fair few words on the issue of relationships. Some of them I can laugh about now, but some of them were hard to swallow at the time. My course was set on a Christian man, as I believed Christians are aware of their need to change to be more like Jesus, and heaven knows we all need to be willing to change. I thank God that he held me to this resolve, even though it was sorely tested at times, especially as there seemed to be a serious lack of "decent" Christian men.

Saturday evening after a busy week at work, my housemate has gone out with her fiancée for the day, and I am at home, cleaning our flat. "I am on a bit of a low" would be an understatement. Feeling that I am the babysitter, or the meeting-goer, but wondering where the fun is in life? I ring my parents for our weekly catch up chat, and perhaps looking for a bit of TLC (Tender Loving Care). My dad answers the phone, which is unusual. We chat for a while, then the barb goes in: "Can't you even find a fella to take you out on a Saturday night?" It led to one of those nights when I buried my head in the pillow crying, asking God if he was never going to give me a husband.

My Dad had a knack at this. My parents had come to visit me and were attending my church with me on a Sunday morning. The Pastor announced that they were going to take up an offering for a visiting African Pastor, who needed the price of seven cows to pay for his wife. My dad leant over and whispered in my ear, "Will they find you a husband, if I give them the price of seven cows?" I am sure it was meant to be amusing, but my confidence took another knock.

So near but so far

"God has told us who you are going to marry. Would you like us to tell you who it is?" some well-meaning Christian friends told me.

"No, thank you very much," I replied very firmly. I knew exactly who they were going to name, and I also knew I definitely was not going to marry him! However, for a couple of months he plied me with anonymous romantic gestures: roses on Valentine's Day; some chocolates; and a cassette tape from the musical "South Pacific" (which includes the song, "I am going to wash that man right out of my hair"!). Although I should have enjoyed the attention, I felt somewhat uneasy. But eventually he asked me out to dinner, and other friends suggested I just go and enjoy the night out. So, I duly got all dressed up and ready for him to come to my house at the appointed time. He came, and said he needed to talk to me. "This has never happened to me before Sally, but God has not given me the money to take you out to dinner." All dressed up and nowhere to go! But I hadn't made all that effort for nothing, so off we went in my car, and I paid for us to have dinner together. Conversation was a little stilted, and in the following days, I reflected how sad it was that he didn't have friends he could have borrowed some money from, rather than spiritualising it. One thing I knew for sure, God is not poor.

A few years later, I did fall head over heels in love. This tall, young man with a lovely Welsh accent was being trained for leadership in the church. Little did he know the time and prayer I invested into him. Every time he was contributing in the church meeting I had his back, so to speak. Socially, we spent time together in a group, and we were very good friends. One day he popped the question, no, not THE question, "Sally, will you come with me to help me buy the double bed for my new house?" You can imagine the dreams that triggered in my mind! However, he seemed to be totally oblivious of my feelings for him. Then, one day, he came to my house and invited me to go on a date – all my prayers were being answered. I found out later that one of the senior leaders in the church had told him to open his eyes to see what was in front of him – so at least the senior leader thought I was "good enough."

A couple of dates later, I wondered if he was ashamed of me, as he didn't even hold my hand. I suppose I shouldn't have been surprised when he arrived at my house again only a couple of weeks into the relationship. "Sally, I asked God that my love for you would grow really quickly, if you were the right girl for me, and it hasn't, so you obviously aren't the right one." I was devastated. There had been no confession of any feelings on his side at the initial ask, so how could he have asked God for his love for me to grow really quickly – what love?

The same evening I sat opposite him in a prayer meeting at church, trying to put on a brave face. The wound felt deep, but then I believed God gave me encouragement from a story in the Bible. Just as Abraham was willing to lay Isaac on the altar, so I had to lay down the relationship, but God would resurrect it, in the same way that he provided an alternative sacrifice for Isaac (Genesis 22:9-13). However, three months later he started dating a friend of mine in the church, a single Mum with two children, and very quickly they became engaged. The wedding invitation arrived. "God, how can I go, how can I be pleased for them when my heart is still aching?" Yet in usual style, God was very gracious, and on the day, it was just like he gave me an anaesthetic, and I could celebrate the day with them. The downside was that it took a few years for me to regain my confidence that I could hear God speaking to me.

Courting Solomon Islands' style

Matchmaking Solomon Islands' style involves extended family contacts and introductions, and Gibson benefitted from this. Whilst at high school on his island, Gibson had a cousin sister (female cousins in the Solomon Islands are referred to as cousin sisters and male cousins as cousin brothers) at Bible College on the main Island, and she "introduced" him to one of her friends. They started to exchange letters, and in my day, they would have been called Pen Pals. However, through the letter writing, the friendship developed into something a little more romantic, possibly similar to Internet dating in Western society.

With the lack of funding to continue his education after his father's death, Gibson made the bold move to go over to the main island to find work. Fortunately, his brother Reuben was leading the youth ministry in a church in Honiara, so it offered Gibson a safe port of call in what was new territory for him. An added benefit was that the letter-writing friend was also a member of the same youth ministry. However, whilst attending the youth group activities, they never exchanged more than a personal "Hello" to each other. May be this was due to youthful embarrassment around showing any interest in the opposite sex, especially in a culture where husbands and wives don't even hold hands in public. Plus, the older members of the church congregation kept a hawk eye on the behaviour of the youth. In time, the letter writing also ceased, probably because it seemed strange to write letters to someone you were seeing regularly, albeit within a group. Gibson did not see or hear from this friend when he moved back to his island, until she turned up at his office in Auki a couple of years later, and tearfully accused him: "I've heard you're engaged to be married?" She thought there was a 'promise' between them, so was he a heart breaker, or was it just young love? There is a happy ending to her story, as she is married now (but not to Gibson!) with her own family.

The Hot Bread Kitchen

The whispering behind hands and the sly nudges of his colleagues at the Hot Bread Kitchen (like an English bakery) in Honiara made Gibson aware that something was being planned, but he had no idea what. Not until he found himself locked in the back locker room with one of the young girls. The two of them stood there in awkward silence. It would be no use pounding on the door, as that would just have increased the merriment of those on the other side of the door. Whether the young men became bored of the joke, or the shop became busy and customers demanded attention, we will never know, but Gibson and the young girl were relieved to hear the key turn in the lock. The whole plot to make sure that Gibson had some romantic experience fell decidedly flat, when the colleagues found out that nothing had happened behind the locked door, not even a sneaky kiss – what an anticlimax.

It's time

"Nudge, nudge, wink, wink, look at Gibson and Jemima, they seem to be getting on very well," sniggered some of the young people. Gibson had returned home for Christmas and his brother Reuben had brought a group of the youth home for Christmas. One evening, the youth group went to sing at a neighbouring village church, and Gibson and a young lady found much to talk about on the walk along the road, bringing up the rear of the party. An attraction sparked between the two of them, and it provoked much teasing from others in the group.

"At twenty-five years old it is time he married," agreed Gibson's brother, his uncle, and his mother, all of whom had a part to play in this. The attraction between Gibson and Jemima provided a great springboard for this to happen – they were saved from a marriage proposal with someone they had never met. So, in Solomon Islands tradition, Jemima's parents were invited to a meeting, to discuss the possibility of a marriage arrangement.

Following the meeting, there is a period of time when the girl's family consider the proposal before they respond to the boy's family. This attractive young girl of course aroused feelings in Gibson, as she would in any other virile young man. Plus, being the dutiful son that he was, he would have complied with the marriage arrangement. However, the miracles of travelling he had seen in his life already, and his custom of practising preaching in English to the trees and the birds on the beach, made him believe that his horizons lay beyond the Solomon Islands. He knew God had something different in store for him, and he certainly did!

Chapter 7

A Growing Relationship

The meeting through English eyes

If you had been sitting with me on the balcony of that wooden house on stilts, you would have seen the flashes of colour as the parrots flew overhead and heard the wind rustling the coconut palms. You might also have heard my heart pounding in nervous anticipation. I'm pretending to read, but keeping a secret eye on the house opposite. Then down the steps come two men, an older black man, distinguished looking, greying at the temples, and a young black guy, tight curly hair and a smile that lights up his face. So I'm stealing a glance down at the young guy and he makes some comment to his uncle about the parrots flying overhead as an excuse to get a look up at me. Our eyes meet and that moment changed our lives.

That same night, February 14th 2000 (Valentine's Day in the UK), we're sitting on wooden chairs at a wooden table in that house on stilts opposite, with the oil lamp burning. The young black man, me, and our chaperones, the tall black distinguished gentleman and his well-endowed, maternal-looking daughter. And I realise that the young black guy, Gibson, is setting out his credentials as a prospective husband. My mind's racing … wow, this isn't how it works where I come from, yet there's something scarily exciting about it. Perhaps the only way I am going to meet my knight in shining armour is by arrangement. And later that night, I write in my diary, "God, let him be willing to get to know me better."

The meeting through a Solomon Islander's eyes

God often seems to give us an inkling of something, without giving us any of the details. He told Abram, "Go from your country, your people and your father's household to the land I will show you" (Genesis 12:1). Abram had to go, before God showed him the land. Gibson had an inkling that God had something special for him, but he did not know what. The two weeks had passed and there had been no response about the marriage proposal from the girl's family on Gibson's Island. Then out of the blue, his Uncle Jephlet sent a note via a truck driver. It read: "Come rains or storm, earthquake or tornado, you must come and visit me." This was Islands' speak for "I want to introduce you to a girl." So with heart beating, he arranged to travel the couple of hours truck journey down to his Uncle's village.

On arrival, his Uncle met him, ushered him into his house and proceeded to "story" Solomon's style about anything and everything. Eventually Gibson broached the subject of the letter.

"Did you bring me here to introduce me to a girl, Uncle?" After some more beating around the bush, his uncle confirmed that there was indeed a lady he would like to introduce him to. "She is teaching at the school and she will be back home at the house opposite after school." Then he dropped the bombshell, "She's a white!" Gibson blanched (as much as a black person can!), and quickly pointed out to his Uncle that no one in his family had married a white person, and he certainly did not think he was the right candidate to be the first.

His Uncle, however, had already decided that this would be a good match, and talked to Gibson persuasively about the possibility of the relationship. "Son," he said, "I want you to meet her, and if she accepts you, then I believe God has a future for you together. If she rejects you, then you will be released from the proposal. Now go and have a shower, then I will take you for a walk." So Gibson found himself going for a walk with his Uncle, nervously glancing up at this white woman on the balcony.

At the meeting in the evening, Gibson's eyes sparkled, as he told me of the miracles he had seen God do in his life.

Boldly, he reasoned that despite all the differences between us, such as age, culture and education, if God had done it before, he could certainly do it again – perhaps I was the lady God had for him.

Courting!

So it was on that first night that the relationship was born. The following evening, the next clandestine meeting took place. We were allowed to talk together in the house I was staying in, with the maternal-looking daughter keeping guard on the balcony outside. These meetings had to take place after dark (6 pm all-year round in the Solomon Islands), to stop any gossip starting in the village.

At this meeting, I was able to explain my position to Gibson. "In my culture, we need to get to know each other to see if we want to spend the rest of our lives together." From the western perspective, this was quite a conservative proposal, where outside of Christian circles, experimenting with sexual compatibility is advocated before entering into a marriage contract. However, I read a story recently, that helped me understand how we are influenced by our cultures: "A certain young lady from India was to be married to a man she didn't know. One day she received a letter from her fiancé, designed to acquaint her with him prior to the wedding. But the bride-to-be returned the letter unopened, saying she believed love should be developed after marriage, not before. 'When we are born,' she wrote, 'we don't get to choose our mother, father, brothers and sisters, yet we learn to live with them and to love them. So it is with a husband or wife.'" These two viewpoints are literally worlds apart.

Gibson broke the tradition to win his prize, but not without many challenges! The school I was working at was midway between Gibson's village and my home base in the town of Auki. At weekends, I would go back down to Auki by truck, sometimes waiting a couple of hours to get a truck ride back again on a Monday morning. Gibson started to come down some weekends to visit. He used to stay with relatives in the small town, until one night he found himself locked out. "We don't like the fact that you are spending time with Sally unchaperoned, it is not good for our family's reputation." Shunned by his extended family, but also bravely, for my sake, trying to join in with the activities of the group of white Voluntary Service Overseas (VSO) volunteers based in Auki.

There were good times, fun trips to the beach, as one of the volunteers had use of a truck, and an occasional evening meal out at a local café, "Louisa's", where the most delicious fish curry was served. There were also some bumps along the way, as might be expected. "Sally, can you give me some money for my art materials?" Gibson asked me one evening. All my alarm bells started ringing and westerners' warnings echoed in my ears – "He probably just wants to marry a rich white woman." However, communication and honesty were integral parts of our relationship, and as obstacles arose, we talked and worked them out together.

With family and cultural pressures weighing on him, it was probably not surprising, that by the beginning of March, Gibson was already seeking a commitment from me. "Sally, either you have the peace of God about our future together, or you don't."

"Whoa, Gibs" I said, using the shortened version of his name I have used since that time. "I am only just getting to know you, it is too soon for me to make this decision about the rest of my life." But there was no doubting his commitment to me. At the end of March, we drove up to Gibs' village in my project truck, for me to meet his family for the first time. What a wonderful welcome I received, as I was embraced into the family. Village life was very simple, no electricity; water from a standpipe in the middle of the village; and toileting in the bush – except before my arrival, Gibs had built me a toilet in the village – a great romantic act in my eyes!

Is this love?

The greeting I had become used to over the months in the Solomon Islands, was "How old are you? Are you married? How many children do you have?" Very unconventional questions to a western lady, and if I admitted that I wasn't married, and I didn't have children, the next question was "Why not?" My answer now tripped easily off my tongue, but it came from the heart: "I want to marry a man who loves God and loves me, and I haven't met him yet." Now, to my amazement, I seemed to have met this man. The smile that lit up his face came from his deep love and passion for God, that shaped his life and flowed out of him to everyone he met. His attention and commitment to me couldn't be questioned, and how I loved the wooing of his skilful guitar playing.

So, did Gibs love me, or was it a commitment to an arrangement, believing that the love would grow? He recalls his first impression was that I too had a beautiful smile, plus lovely legs. It's a good job he mentioned the smile first, as I wrote in an earlier chapter that when my Mum complimented me on my legs, I said I would be OK if I wore a bag over my head! As our relationship developed, he noted more of my character and qualities: "You spoke of your love for God, and you were kind to everyone. Your maturity gave you a confidence above that of the young Island girls I knew. Your enthusiasm and love of life were contagious, and made me excited at the thought of sharing life with you."

Where does our future lie?

The Department for International Development (DFID)

PRIMARY EDUCATION

PROJECT MANAGER

HONIARA, SOLOMON ISLANDS

The advertisement appeared at the end of March 2000. The job was made for me. It was the project I was working on as a volunteer, and I had all the skills required for the post from my previous experience in the UK. Gibs and I talked about it, and I gave him my commitment: "I should get an interview for the post, in which case they will need to fly me home to England. This will give me the opportunity to speak to my parents about our relationship, which I really want to do in order to honour them."

However, this was another occasion when it turned out that I was running ahead of God, trying to tell him the plan for my life. The anticipated interview wasn't offered! It didn't make sense at the time, but the Bible tells us that his ways are higher than our ways, and his thoughts than our thoughts (Isaiah 55:9). My hopes dashed, we started a new chapter.

After the Easter break I was posted at another school in a village in the south of the Island, called Laulana. This increased the distance between Gibs and I, so he decided to move down to the town, where he rented a room and started a sign writing and T-shirt printing business with a friend. He was quickly learning romantic western ways – coming back from my school village on a Friday, I would find a flower on my desk, which warmed my heart. I once questioned a deputy headteacher I was working with, "Why don't you give your wife flowers to show her how much you appreciate her?" His retort came back, "She wouldn't thank me for it, as you can't eat a flower. She would ask me why I hadn't brought a fish to feed the family."

Gibs' consideration of my needs, and his attempts to woo me in line with my culture, were a continuing challenge for him. It was natural to me that we should hold hands as we walked down the street, but unbeknown to me, he had to ignore people's comments and staring, and avoid their gaze, as culturally this wasn't approved of. Even husbands and wives don't hold hands in the street in the Solomon Islands.

Permission sought

With the England trip not happening, still wanting to honour my Mum and Dad, Gibs wrote to them asking for their permission to marry me. The proposed wedding date was 16th September, my Mum and Dad's wedding anniversary.

Gibs' letter (verbatim) sent by airmail:

3rd May 2000

Dear Ron and Doreen,

Best wishes and Regards from the Solomons to you wishing you God's blessing through this communication.

I'm Gibs, writing this note to you. I know your Daughter Sally has already mentioned to you about myself and my family. It is a great honour indeed to express my heart to you concerning the situation we both experience at this present time.

I know from my friend Sally that you would really like to know me. There's nothing much more for me to say concerning myself and family because I know your Daughter has already told everything to you.

With regards to our friendship, I would like to know what you think. Are you in favour of our Agreement or not as we would both like to marry at any appropriate time the Lord allows.

From my own aspect from the very first contact I had with your Daughter, I experience that our Relationship continues to build up as time goes on. We both experience that our Relationship is very strong and firm.

The way I feel with your Daughter, absolutely, let me say to you, I truly love your Daughter and I want to do the best I can to assist her in any way she might need me to do. Despite our age difference, I promise to love Sally till death separates us.

I respect your decision, 'cos you got the right to say something to me and even my family so that we'll know that you accept me to marry your Daughter or not.

I now looking forward to your Reply after receiving this note of mine.

With love & Regards,
God bless
Love ... Gibs

My Dad's reply to me (he sent a separate letter to Gibs):

18th May 2000

My dear Sally,

... Now to you my girl!!! Go ahead with all my blessing, but! if things should not work out, you will always have me to rely on. (Don't show this to Gibs). I feel you have found the simple way of life with few complications and say God bless you, you have followed and given Him everything and I now feel he is returning some of this. Too old now for me to change. Would like to think of the two of you on the 16th Sept. It has done us proud for 49 years, but don't think we can make the journey. Have it in mind though that if you both want to visit, we can help with expenses. Age difference, well my Mum and Dad had this and had some problems, but he can look after you when you are old!!!

I am writing a separate letter to Gibs and Reuben. (Threatening them with dire trouble if they let you down, Ha! Ha!)

Go for it girl and May God bless you both fruitfully.

Lots and Lots of Love,
Dad

The engagement

With my Dad giving us the go ahead, the end of May found us in Gibs' village again, along with a VSO friend from Holland. I had shared another western tradition with Gibs, so when we managed to steal a swim together in the sea, he asked the crucial question, "Sally, will you marry me?" Fortunately my response was affirmative, as the family were gathering to present us with flower garlands and for one of Gibs' Uncles who was a Pastor, to pray for us to celebrate our engagement.

No slow, slow, quick quick slow with our relationship, it was all full speed ahead. During the week following our engagement, we heard that there was a VSO volunteering opportunity at the teacher training college on the main Island to start in July. What an opportunity – I relished the idea of lecturing in the teacher training college, and practically, VSO would provide us with married accommodation on the main Island rather than expecting us to share a house with two other volunteers. This was quickly followed by contact with one of my dear friends in England, saying she would come and visit me in June – my very first English visitor. So we decided to bring the wedding forward to the 29th June, when my friend could be there for me, and we would travel with her back to the main Island for her to fly home and for us to go on a honeymoon.

The parting

The wedding plans were going ahead full throttle. Our friend Pastor David was going to marry us and the banns were being read. I was looking for material to have my wedding dress made, and we had booked a panpipe band to come and play at the wedding feast. I was getting a little alarmed however, that everyone we met, Gibs invited to the wedding. Nothing like the English idea of an invited number of guests, here everyone was invited and I wasn't sure how we were going to feed them all!

Suddenly, metaphorically, a tornado struck. On Monday 5th June, we heard that there had been a political coup the day before on the main Island. This was followed by the news that all international flights had been cancelled. Part of VSO's commitment to its volunteers is that they will fly them out of the country if they need medical care, so talk started about evacuation. I managed to contact our in-country manager to ask if Gibs would be allowed to come with me, but the answer was "No." I then went to see Pastor David to ask if he would marry us before I had to leave, but his words were even more upsetting: "Sally, I can't marry you two before you have to leave, as you may never see each other again." I remember walking back from this meeting very upset and meeting a young man from the Assemblies Of God Church I was attending. When I explained the situation, he said to me, "Never mind Sally, our Lord Jesus may return before then." I have to say it took all my self-control not to give him a right hook!

I walked into the room where Gibs was doing his sign writing and T-shirt printing, and sobbing and shaking, shared the news of the two decisions with him. He says this is when the light dawned on him, "She really does love me!" Within a week, on Sunday 11th June, we were at the landing strip near the town of Auki, saying our goodbyes. VSO had chartered a flight to fly their volunteers from Malaita Province to Australia, via Papua New Guinea, and then onto England. The landing strip is near a beach. Gibs and I sat on the beach together holding hands, waiting for the chartered plane to land. "What are your dreams and hopes for the future, Gibs?" I asked him, desperately trying to hold onto our future together. But how does an Island boy who lives in a literal world, project into a future he cannot imagine? And so we parted.

Chapter 8

Till Death Us Do Part

Separation

Gibs became smaller and smaller until the sight of him faded away completely. As we flew away from Malaita Province on the small-chartered aeroplane, I did not know when I would see my Love again. My house-share volunteer, Rita, and I decided to take the opportunity of spending a few days sightseeing in Australia before returning to England. But my heart was heavy, as my repeated calls to the Solomon Islands were unsuccessful – lines were down, and Gibs and I were well and truly separated. My hope was failing, and then I saw it, in a boutique – my wedding dress. A simple, white dress, in my mind, Island-style, a patterned bodice and a flared cheesecloth skirt. It did not bear the exorbitant price tag of English wedding dresses, but for me, it was the costly test of my faith. I bought it, refusing to believe the words of the Pastor who would not marry us before I left, "...as you may never see each other again..."

Arriving back in England at Heathrow Airport, my older, and of course wiser brother met me and took me to stay at their home for a couple of nights. My sister-in-law cautioned me: "Sally, is there really any future in this relationship? Gibs is much younger than you, he doesn't have your education, and he comes from a totally different culture. It surely won't work." But I had waited many long years to meet this man I believed God was giving to me, and my mind was set on how we could be reunited.

Before leaving for the Solomon Islands, I had closed chapters of my life, so to speak – resigned a high-powered job; sold my house in West Yorkshire; and given most of my possessions away. Therefore, on my return, I went back to live with my long-suffering parents in Sussex. It's quite a call to take a forty+ year old who has been away for more than twenty years back into your home – and a lovesick one, at that. Fortunately, after a couple of weeks, I obtained some temporary work accompanying a group of French students on their trips out. This brought in a little income, plus it gave me something else to occupy my mind. But it was tough. I had questions for God: "Why would you let me meet the man of my dreams in my forties, then let us be separated with no knowledge of when we could be reunited?" I didn't get an answer. On one occasion, my parents had visitors, and I heard the news that there were still no flights in or out of the Solomon Islands, which meant no mail could get through. I went into the garden shed for privacy, and cried.

Meanwhile, Gibs continued with his work in the town of Auki. Well-meaning folks around him were warning him, "Forget her, Gibs. Now she has returned to England, you won't hear from her again." He felt secure with his own people in his own country, but he also had the strength to resist the negativity. Just as he had known that it was right to marry me, he now knew that if we were meant to be together, God would make a way.

Contact restored

Four long, silent weeks followed, then a breakthrough came. Rita, my house-share volunteer, let me know that she had had contact by e-mail with a friend on the main Island. This was my opportunity. Rita arranged for me to e-mail a letter to her friend and ask her to send it over on the boat to Gibs on his Island. I wrote, "I am missing you so much Darling. Please go over to Honiara (on the main Island) and telephone me at my parents' house. Don't worry about bringing anything with you. I am going to try to make a way for you to come over to England." I sent the e-mail, then, metaphorically, I held my breath. Would this plan work? Would the letter even get to him? If it did get to him, would his family allow him to go to the main Island? Would he find a way to telephone me?

Gibs was walking through the town of Auki, when someone who worked at the post office hailed him: "Hey Bro, iu garem letter blong iu long Post Ofis (you have a letter at the Post Office)." Excitedly, Gibs ran to the Post Office to collect the letter. He tore it open and read it right there in the street. Then he didn't waste any time. He went straight to speak to the friend that he worked with, showed him the letter, and told him that he needed to travel back to his village that same day. An abrupt end to a business partnership!

The wheels were now in motion. A truck was travelling north, he got a ride and arrived at his village in the early evening as darkness fell. He called his Mum and his older brother Reuben aside and showed them the letter. The words I had written assured them that I was serious about our future together, but he was Mum's baby. He was about to set off on the adventure of a lifetime, if it all worked out, when would she see him again? Yet all Mums want the best for their children, so with tears in her eyes, they prayed for him, and sent him back to Auki on a truck in the early hours of the morning. The rest of the village was totally unaware of what had happened that night. Sitting in the back of that truck as they travelled through the night under the stars, Gibs felt a mixture of excitement and total dependence on God. The vastness of the heavens seemed to reflect the enormity of what lay ahead of him.

Early morning found him on the boat to Honiara. In keeping with Solomon Island's hospitality, when he arrived, he went by bus to the house of a friend, Peter, who worked for Solomon Islands Telekom. When Gibs had lived in Honiara, he had done sign writing with Peter, but Peter knew nothing of Gibs' relationship with me. So, Gibs told his story, and explained that he needed to make an international call to England. "No problem" was Peter's response, "We will go to my office at night and I will connect the call for you."

Back in England, I was enjoying my temporary post chaperoning the group of French students on their trips out.

This particular day we had visited the historic town of Arundel in West Sussex. As I got off the bus and walked towards my parents' bungalow, I was surprised to see my Mum standing on the doorstep. She couldn't have any news for me I reasoned, as it was mid-afternoon, which meant that it was the early hours of the morning in the Solomon Islands. But I was wrong! She could hardly contain her excitement, "He's rung, Gibs has rung." It turned out that Peter had taken Gibs to his office about 2am and Gibs and my Mum had talked for a long time. My Mum was delighted to have her first chat ever with him, I was a little jealous. However, Mum had arranged for me to ring him back at 11pm our time. The hours passed so slowly, but finally the clock struck eleven and the call was connected. Hearing his voice again was like music to my ears. There is the slight delay in speech that needs negotiating, but it amazed me that even though he was thousands of miles away, I still felt that I could have reached out and touched him.

Arrangements

Phone calls and faxes went back and forth as we tried to make arrangements for Gibs to come over to England. It was not straightforward. "I have sent the money for your fare Gibs, go and buy your ticket," I told him excitedly in a call. But sadly he returned my call, "There's not enough money Sally, the exchange rate has fallen." A second transfer was made. Now Gibs had to renew his passport, as he only had two months left before it expired. For my part, I was e-mailing the British High Commissioner to get verification that I had worked in the Solomon Islands as a volunteer and that our relationship was bona fide.

There were challenges every step of the way. My fax to Gibs on 25th July 2000 read, "Qantas in London confirms that there are no seats on the flight from Honiara, Solomon Islands to Brisbane, Australia (the route to England) on 1st August. Please try other dates." Then there was also the difficulty that he would need to spend a couple of nights in

Brisbane, before he could get a connecting flight onto London Heathrow. As usual, God made provision. The strategic friend, Peter, was not only the means of international phone calls and faxes, but he also had friends who lived in Brisbane, whom he had met through the church. Eventually the date was booked. Gibs would fly to Australia on 15th August, and spend one night there with the friends in Brisbane, George and Sue, now very good friends of ours as well. Then on 16th August, he started on the long journey to London Heathrow, an amazing feat to travel so far on his own, negotiating two international transfers. With some trepidation, he was literally stepping out of one world and into another.

In the meantime, in England, much to my amazement, I was contacted by a former colleague. "Will you come and do some consultancy work in the Early Years Department of my local authority?" Head hunted? That didn't happen to people like me, and the consultancy fees offered seemed exorbitant, but the income was greatly needed. My concern was, could I prove my worth?

My Pastors and very close friends in Yorkshire, Ian and Julie, kindly said that I could lodge with them. The arrangements to bring Gibs over from the Solomons, were going hand in hand with the arrangements in England for our wedding. One evening I spoke to Ian: "As my Pastor and my very dear friend, will you do me the honour of marrying Gibs and I?" I was devastated by his answer: "I'm not sure. I don't even know Gibs, so I don't know if I can join you in a marriage covenant." I cried myself to sleep that night, but the next day, I told him with firm resolve, "If you love me, you will have to love Gibs as well," and this seemed to persuade him – or God convicted him! The plan was to marry down at my parents' home in West Sussex, and my Mum was doing a stalwart job of making the practical arrangements.

The arrival

The week beginning 14th August, I went down to stay with my parents, to make the final arrangements for the wedding. My Auntie Hazel (my godmother) took me on a shopping trip to buy me a veil. "Auntie Hazel," I confided in her, "What will I do if when I see him again I decide I don't love him?" (Pre-wedding nerves were obviously setting in!) Having been through a failed marriage herself, her answer was firm and clear, "You will tell him you're sorry and send him straight back on a plane to the Solomon Islands."

But by 6am on Thursday 17th August, I made my way to Arrivals at Heathrow airport, and I was dancing from one foot to the other in sheer excited anticipation. People had warned me that there might be problems with immigration, but seeing on the monitor that the flight had arrived, I stood at the arrivals barrier straining to see his face. Then the announcement came over the tannoy: "Will the person meeting Gibson Ben come to the Meeting Point." An Immigration Officer was waiting for me at the Meeting Point and he escorted me upstairs. He asked me about meeting Gibs, and I told him excitedly that we were getting married on Saturday. "Oh no you're not," he replied, "He hasn't got the right papers." As thoughts flew through my mind of documentaries I had seen, where people were put straight back on return flights to their country, the Immigration Officer did add, "Would you like to see him?" Of course I gave an enthusiastic "Yes, please." And there was Gibs, sitting on one of the stark plastic seats. Not much of a welcome to England, being detained by Immigration, after travelling for over thirty hours! We showed the Immigration Officer the paperwork we had, including a fax from the British High Commissioner in the Solomon Islands, confirming that Gibs could enter the country for six months on a visitor's visa. The Immigration Officer looked at the papers and said, "This is highly irregular. I will have to go and show the paperwork to the Chief Immigration Officer." As he walked away, I grasped Gibs' hand and prayed: "Lord, you are the Author of this relationship. We have done all we can, now we need you to make a way please." We watched nervously, rather than in faith, as the Immigration Officer returned. "OK," he said, "He can have a visitor's visa, and you can get married, but he must leave the country again within six months and obtain a visa in order to return to England." We breathed a grateful sigh of relief.

There was more waiting around for his passport to be stamped, then we escaped to my car in the multi-storey car park, and in the safety of the car we had a kiss and a cuddle – all my doubts had disappeared! We set off to drive down to my parents, stopping at a roadside rest stop for some breakfast, and onto the register office to collect the marriage license. Arriving at my parents' bungalow about 10 am, first introductions were made. Gibs had not had much sleep, as he was fascinated by the movies on the aeroplanes, so after lunch he went for a sleep. As the afternoon stretched into the evening, my Mum said to me, "Don't you think you should wake him?" But I decided to let him sleep, which he did right through to Friday morning.

Preparations

Gibs had taken me seriously about not bringing much with him and he had arrived with a small rucksack. Consequently, on the Friday morning, we set off to the local town of Worthing to buy his wedding suit, shoes etc. It was an eventful trip. The department store assistant asked me, "What is his inside leg measurement?" She seemed somewhat floored when I replied that I had no idea. Then Gibs needed the toilet, so I took him to the Public Conveniences on the seafront. "What happens inside?" he asked me, looking bewildered. I declared that I couldn't go into the Gents with him and he would have to navigate his own way when he got in there. We did eventually arrive back at my parents' bungalow with all the kit he needed for the next day.

Pastor Ian and Julie arrived in the evening ready for the wedding rehearsal at the local free church. We came to the part in the service where the groom is told that he can kiss the bride – Gibs was really flustered! Remember that they don't show affection in public in the Solomon Islands. "Don't worry Pastor Ian, it's fine; you can just leave it out."

The wedding day

The wedding day dawned bright and beautiful, which was a good job, as my sleeveless dress and open-toed sandals were in the style of a tropical wedding. Two of my fellow volunteers in the Solomon Islands, Ken and Andy, had also returned to England and we had asked them to be Gibs' Best Men, as they were the only people he knew in England apart from me. They arrived on the Saturday morning and took Gibs round to my Auntie's bungalow to get ready for the wedding. Julie came round to blow dry my hair for me, and Mum had arranged for her local hairdresser to fit my fresh flower headdress. Finally the time had come, and I was walking down the aisle to meet the man of my dreams.

It was a small gathering and a simple ceremony; we had written our vows using words from the book of Ruth (1:16) in the Bible: "Where you go I will go, and where you stay I will stay. Your people will be my people and your God my God."

I remember seeing my Mum, who never cried, wipe a tear from her eyes – I think she marvelled that she was finally seeing this day. When we came to the part where Ian would say "You can now kiss the bride", he went ahead and said it, and Gibs gave me such a smacker that he nearly knocked me off my feet! I had chosen Caribbean style music (the nearest match I could find for the Solomon Islands at the time) for the end of the service and I literally danced down the aisle hand in hand with Gibs as we left the church.

The reception took place in the upstairs room of my parents' local pub. I had panicked when my Mum had told me we were having a roast beef dinner, as food in the

Solomon Islands is eaten with a spoon and I wasn't sure how confident Gibs would feel using a knife and fork. Therefore, my Mum arranged for there to be choices, and I plumped for the chicken curry for Gibs and I, confident that we could eat that with a spoon. What I didn't realise was that Gibs wasn't used to spices, so he barely ate anything, and we ended up getting a Chinese takeaway on our wedding night!

Gibs surprised me again at the wedding reception, when he stood up and made a speech. Somehow, in his small rucksack, he had managed to bring traditional shell money as a gift for my parents. This is a seven-foot string, made up of nine strands of tiny threaded shells, worth about the equivalent of £100. A custom on Gibs' Island of Malaita, was that the groom's family would pay bride price to the girl's family, in the form of traditional shell money. As Gibs explained this to the wedding guests, he "dressed" me in the shell money.

After the reception, we were able to walk through the village in the beautiful sunshine, back to my parents' bungalow. We had cups of tea and wedding cake, before guests journeyed home, and we drove the short distance to my Auntie's bungalow, which she had offered us the use of for our wedding night. The next day, Sunday, we went round to say goodbye to my parents, before we set off to drive back to Yorkshire to begin married life together.

The Wedding

Traditional Shell Money

Chapter 9

Married Life

Fiction or reality?

I was singing under the coconut palms with a group of pikininis. "Do you think the streets in England are paved in gold?"

"Yes," they answered me in an enthusiastic chorus.

Then I asked, "Do you believe there are staircases that move that you can ride upstairs on?"

"No," they all shook their heads and looked at me as though I had lost my senses. When you live in a very literal world, you believe what you are told, and it is hard to imagine things that are beyond your experience. Fast forwarding, as we drove up the motorway the day after our wedding, Gibs was surprised to see so many green fields, and then he asked me, "Does everyone in England have a gun?" Surprised, I asked him, "Where did you get that idea?" He explained that his high school often showed videos as fundraisers – students would pay to watch the film and the money would be used to buy materials for the school. These were usually films like Rambo, which had coloured his expectations of the West.

A honeymoon would have to wait. Two days after our wedding, I returned to work – we needed to have some money coming in. A dear friend had gone on a six-week holiday to America, and she had offered us the use of her house. The first evening I arrived home after work, I noticed that the lounge curtains were still closed. I thought it was just a cultural thing – Gibs wasn't used to curtains, but when it continued for the next two weeks, I had to ask the question. "Gibs, is there a reason why you aren't opening the curtains, wouldn't you like to let some daylight in?"

"Yes Sally, I do miss the sunshine, but what if someone sees me and says I shouldn't be here?"

"Sweetheart, you have as much right to be here as anyone else, you were given permission to enter the country." I don't think I appreciated how daunting it was to have black skin when living among so many fair skinned people. However, the following week he boldly ventured out to the local shop, and as we were living in Dewsbury (West Yorkshire), he saw that there were many other non-white faces on our streets.

Adjustments

Soon after our wedding, a friend of mine in her late thirties married a man also in his late thirties. We were chatting on the phone, and she confided in me, "It's been difficult to adjust to married life, probably because we have both lived the single life for so long." I hope I made understanding noises, whilst secretly wondering at the fact that marrying Gibs felt like putting my hand into a perfectly fitting glove. Was this because Gibs was still in his mid-twenties, or just because he is such a wonderful man? So it was that one Saturday, not long after we were married, we were having a lie-in, and I had tears of joy running down my face. I was full of wonder, that here I was at last, married to this gorgeous man, who loved me, and even thought I was beautiful – perhaps I had inherited some of the good looks of my Mum and Dad! In a conference meeting in the UK, I heard the whisper of God in my spirit, "I will give you the nineteen years difference between you and Gibs to live all over again." I am not sure exactly what that meant, but oh the joy of sharing things together that were firsts for him: going on a swing in the park; seeing the fireworks on Bonfire Night; sledging down a hill in a snowfall. The simple things of life that we both relish together.

For Gibs, there were so many adjustments, it was even hard for me to understand them all. He was suddenly thrust into a world where you needed to carry a wallet and keys around (and there were many occasions when he misplaced them!). He couldn't understand why people didn't greet each other in the street, and when we visited a huge indoor shopping mall, the sheer number of people and the huge choice of goods overwhelmed him. Sometimes I was not as patient as I should have been. We were standing together in the queue in a busy fish and chip shop in Dewsbury town. It was our turn to be served and I asked him, "Do you want salt and vinegar on your fish and chips, Gibs?" He hesitated, looking confused (they don't have vinegar in the Solomon Islands on their reef fish and sweet potato chips), and feeling under pressure from the other people in the queue, I didn't wait for his answer, but made the decision for him. I can try to excuse myself, by reasoning that it was probably a relief to him, as there were so many decisions to make in this new environment, but I still had a lot of growing to do in my understanding of our cultural differences.

God's provision

God's provision was truly amazing. Helping Gibs acclimatise was not left to me alone. Our dear friends and Pastors, Ian and Julie, held a barbecue at their home for us to celebrate our marriage and for Gibs to meet friends from the church. It was at this gathering that Gibs first met John and Barbara. John had previously suffered a stroke and consequently was no longer working. "Gibs, how would you like me to come and take you out once a week whilst Sally is at work, to help you get to know Yorkshire?" Gibs hesitantly agreed, little knowing that as John helped him over the weeks to understand and navigate life in England, he would become an English father to Gibs. Barbara reports that, prior to my time in the Solomon Islands, she felt I was out of her class, knowing that I had been a headteacher. But our friendship as couples developed over the years, and turned out to be a God-joining, as John and Barbara are still special friends twenty years later, and we both count them as family. They have stood with us, supported us, and believed in us through all the ups and downs across the years.

During my elongated single years, I had read lots of ways of praying for a husband. One of the ones that has stuck in my mind, was to hang a pair of men's trousers at the end of your bed and ask God to fill them! This wasn't something I tried, but I did have some items on my 'wish list', and one of them was a man who could serenade me. Well, God certainly answered that one. As we didn't have our own house to equip when we were first married, we received some generous financial gifts instead of practical gifts, and Gibs had a request: "Sally, could we buy a decent guitar?" How could I refuse, when Gibs' gifted guitar playing and great voice were an answer to my prayer?

At the end of September, the news came through that VSO had decided that it would not be possible for the volunteers to return to the Solomon Islands, so Gibs and I needed another place to live. As usual, our God of over and above came up with the goods. John and Barbara were going on holiday for a week and offered us their house for that week. One night, the telephone rang in the middle of the night. I woke up instantly and knew it was a call from the Solomon Islands, at that time of night. However, waking Gibs was another matter. One of the "gifts" of Islanders, seems to be the ability to sleep like the dead, almost anywhere. When I finally roused him, he was so disorientated, that he got out of bed and walked into the wardrobe, mistaking the wardrobe door for the bedroom door. A memory for our laughter bank to this day.

Our next move was to an en-suite room made available to us in the beautiful and spacious home of some more church friends. We were very blessed, but there were crucial decisions to be made about the future before Gibs' visitor's visa expired. Our conversation and prayers revolved around the major question: are we going to stay in England, or are we going to go back to live in the Solomon Islands? As part of my consultancy work, I had put a project plan together for a government Sure Start programme in Barnsley, and the manager's job was out to advert. The way God guides me is usually through opening and closing doors, so we decided that I would apply for the post and if I was successful, it would be God's confirmation for us to stay in England, and vice versa.

"We would like to offer you the post." The words were music to my ears – what a privilege to write a proposal for a project and then set that project up. We also saw the job offer as God's green light for us to set up home in England. Gibs was not allowed to work in England with his visitor visa, but he volunteered his practical and artistic skills to the Sure Start programme, which added great benefit to my work. Little did we know at the time, that it would also be to our benefit. At the end of the year, we travelled back to the Solomon Islands, where Gibs had to be interviewed at the British High Commissioner's Office in order to obtain a spouse's visa to return to England. The questions were searching: "What does your wife do? What services does her programme provide?" To be honest I don't think most spouses would be able to answer, but due to his volunteering, Gibs was all clued up. So in proud possession of his spouse's visa, we returned to England at the end of December 2000, ready to build our lives together.

God's provision has followed us through the years. I realised that we had outgrown our first small terraced house, when I came home from work to find the lounge taken over by Gibs' sign writing paraphernalia. We moved on to an end-terraced house in Batley, which as the meter reader commented every time he visited, was larger on the inside than it looked from the outside! It had a large kitchen diner which was great for entertaining, and we certainly made the most of it. We have visitor books that bear names from around the world. We 'collected' people like some people collect possessions.

Whilst we were living in Batley, much to my surprise, my very generous cousin passed on an inheritance from my

Auntie, telling us we were more in need of it than he was. Now on visits to the Solomon Islands, accommodation in Gibs' village was tricky to say the least. Gibs' brother would kindly try to vacate a room in his house for us, but his growing family was making this more difficult, and privacy was hard to come by. The generous gift allowed us to have a house built in the village – we named the house 'Jireh Lodge', which means the Lord provides. It provided a holiday place for us to stay, and we hoped that it would also be a source of income for the family.

Our final move to date was to our current house, which has a garden that backs onto a field, which gives Gibs the sense of space that he misses from his beloved Solomon Islands. We have faithfully tithed (the practice of giving 10% of your income away) throughout our lives and we are overwhelmed at how God provides for us in so many ways, as he is our ultimate source. Sitting at my Dad's bedside in his nineties, he proudly told me, "You'll be secure financially when I go, Sally." I didn't want him to speak of his death, but it was true. My half of his inheritance enabled us to pay off our mortgage and invest money to help us in the future. I like to think of him smiling down from heaven saying "I told you so."

Challenges

"Smooth seas do not make skilful sailors" (African Proverb), and "Great relationships aren't great because they have no problems. They're great because both people care enough about the other person to find a way to make it work." In some ways, Gibs and I have faced extra challenges in bringing together two totally different cultures, but we are both very clear that Jesus is the centre of each of our lives individually, and the centre of our marriage. This means that each of us is willing to change (eventually), and that one of the ground rules of our marriage is to forgive one another, just as God forgives each of us. Not that this comes naturally, it takes a lot of work, like climbing a mountain, but the view is certainly worth it at the top!

"Money makes the world go round" – the lyric rings in my ears, and money so often causes stress in relationships. In the early years of our marriage, we were shopping in the town of Batley. "Sally, I have seen some shirts in the charity shop and I would like to get a couple."

"Gibs, you don't really need any more shirts and we have come shopping for other things. Please can you go and buy the paint brushes, I'll buy the food, and we'll meet back here in fifteen minutes." When we met back at the car at the agreed time, I saw in Gibs' hand, the paint brushes and a bag from the charity shop, containing you can guess what! However ridiculous this sounds, I was devastated, to me, he had broken my trust. To my shame, this incident took a couple of days to resolve, as we finally each talked through our feelings.

Fortunately we do have similar values, both appreciating people above things, and both enjoying the simple things in life. Gibs is one of the most generous people I know, and I like to give, but my parents taught me to be careful with money. Gibs once explained to me that in his culture, if someone verbally admires something you are wearing, or a possession you have, it is custom to give that something to them. This caused further upset in the future if it was something I had given to Gibs as a gift. For myself, I find it easy to give something to someone else, but I struggle to spend money on myself – this has been challenging for Gibs, who likes to spoil me with gifts and treat himself when money is available. A friend once described me as frugal, which I did not think was very complimentary!

Having married "a rich white woman", requests from overseas for finance have come thick and fast. Can you help with the cost of building my house? Can you help with my son's wedding costs? Can you buy me some art materials and send them over? For Gibs, the dilemma is that our standard of living in England is much higher than in the

Solomon Islands, and my dilemma is that we cannot be people's source of provision – I was taught that you appreciate things much more when you work for them.

We are learning together! Gibs tries to be open with me about financial requests, and when he tells me he has received a message from a wantok (one talk – someone related in some way), I try to listen and not jump to the conclusion that he or she is asking for something. I think we are getting better at working through it together and deciding upon the best course of action. Most recently, this has been in offering one of our nephews some work that needs doing on our house in the village, so we can pay him for his labour.

Achievements

If pride is a sin, then I need to ask for forgiveness, as I could not be prouder of my husband. Moving from the West to an under developed country involves sacrifices such as having to fetch your water in buckets when the supply is cut off, or trying to read by the light of a kerosene lamp, but it is nothing compared to moving to the West with all its intricacies of modern life. Gibs' achievements range from increasing his confidence, to making his mark in our land. In the early months of our marriage, he moved from being nervous about opening the curtains in case he was seen, to returning a pair of sandals to a shop to exchange them, as they were faulty. His English has improved to the extent that people think he was born in England (in Yorkshire, to be exact, as he has picked up the accent more than me!). He has spoken at church meetings and shared the good news of Jesus on the streets in Dewsbury and in Leeds, something many of us Brits would not dare to do. A red letter day was when he received his British citizenship, and another was the day of his launch concert of 'Orphan Boy', the CD of his songs that he had recorded with the help of a good friend. His artwork has also received acclaim.

A 1-2 combination

"I see you as a one-two combination," was the word of encouragement given to us by another Christian. In boxing, the "one-two combo" is the name given to the combination consisting of two common punches found in boxing – a jab (thrown with the lead hand) followed by the cross (thrown with the back hand). We love it when our gifts are combined, so imagine the joy when the Solomon Star newspaper published my article on Saturday 28th July 2018:

From Village Boy to British Museum

Our own home-grown artist, Gibson Ben, has made his mark in Britain. Gibson grew up in Onebusu village in North Malaita and started off drawing pictures of our native birds and fish, using a stick in the sand, or charcoal from the fire on green banana leaves.

When he moved to Honiara and had access to acrylic paint, he started to develop his own designs. These were influenced by the rich colours of our natural environment. He recreated the patterns of mat weavers, and the shell patterns inlaid by wood carvers.

He has continued developing these vibrant designs since marrying his English wife and going to live in England eighteen years ago. Several visits back to our "Happy Isles" have continued to fuel his passion for our nation and inspire his enthusiasm.

In Britain, he has mainly marketed his work with Pacific Islanders who want a permanent reminder of home.

At the recent setting in of the Solomon Islands High Commissioner in London, Gibson presented two of his paintings as gifts to be displayed in the London office.

Ben Burt, an employee of the British Museum, was present at the London occasion and took an interest in Gibson's paintings. He asked Gibson to e-mail some images. This resulted in his colleague asking to acquire two of them for the British Museum Oceania Collection. So, on Friday 20th July, Gibson and his wife Sally travelled from their home in the North of England to London to deliver the works of art.

Words cannot express their joy as they joined the hundreds of people from many different nations visiting this incredible establishment. Gibson was so thrilled to see the Solomon Island artefacts on display, and to know that his paintings could play a part in this. Gibson said: "Only God could take a village boy to the British Museum. All praise and glory goes to my God who gave me the talent."

Growing our marriage

Gibs' friendly, winning ways and his wisdom have always been something I have admired and learnt from. I was amazed in the early stage of our marriage to listen to him as he counselled friends who were struggling in their marriage relationship. How had he learnt this wisdom? Twenty years on, our latest venture has been to do a marriage coaching course together. One of the tasks was to ask each other one thing we would like to change in our marriage. "I would like to understand our finances better and have my own budget," Gibs told me (no surprise there). It created an opportunity for us to take a good look at our finances and budget them together.

"I would like you to take the initiative to plan our times out together, rather than it always falling to me," I confided in him. What a treat when he took this on board and a couple of weeks later he arranged to take me to the Sky Room at a hotel in Leeds, where we indulged in luxury hot chocolate (the afternoon tea was an exorbitant price!).

Chapter 10

Becoming A Family

Hopes and dreams

"If I can't be a prima ballerina, I want to get married and have children," I announced to anyone who asked me what I wanted to do when I left school. A desire frowned upon by some in the mid 70s, when the women's liberation movement was in full swing. Children have always been a central part of my life, from babysitting in my teens, to training as an early years teacher, and volunteering in children's work in churches over the years. I confess that at one point, despite my strong Christian morals, I was desperate for a child whether I had a husband or not – not that I ever did anything about it!

Gibs had grown up surrounded by children in the tight-knit village community in the Solomon Islands. Plus, there is a high expectation in the Solomon Islands that once a couple are married, they will have children. Gibs and I discussed the possibility of a future together before we were engaged. "You can't marry me in the hope of having children Gibs. There's no reason I know of why I couldn't have children, but our relationship has to be based on us wanting each other, not what we can give each other." I am so glad that we had that conversation before we made a commitment to each other, as otherwise it could have been a big stumbling block as our life together unfolded.

So married life began, and it was a match of a virile twenty-five year old and a forty-four year old with years of pent-up passion! One of the benefits was that contraception was never needed right from the wedding night, as we both shared the hope and dream of having children. Married life was wonderful, but as each month came round, I would lament, "I'm not pregnant." My wonderful husband however, would respond to my monthly dismay with, "Well, at least you know you can still get pregnant."

I was in a church meeting about a year after our wedding, standing next to a friend who was very recently married. I had the distinct thought, "She will be pregnant before you." I believe the Holy Spirit whispers to us, in this case to help me deal with the disappointment. She had conceived on her honeymoon and actually had two children whilst we were still hoping and trying!

There is plenty of advice to be had on increasing chances of conceiving. I think we tried them all, from temperature monitoring to determine ovulation, to me standing on my head after making love to give the sperm the best chance of connecting with the egg! There were some false hopes in the first years of our marriage. One time we were travelling home from the Solomon Islands and I felt sickly. I went to the pharmacy in Brisbane, "What can I take for travel sickness if it's possible I am pregnant?" They recommended ginger tablets. We returned to stay for a few days with my parents before going back up north and my Mum arranged for me to see their GP as I was still feeling under the weather.

"No, you're not pregnant. It can take couples a year or so to become pregnant," the GP gently told me. On another occasion, I really thought, "This is it", and even submitted a pregnancy test to our GP, only to hear that it was negative.

Medical advice is always to try for a decent length of time before seeking help from your GP, but my age was against me and eventually I booked an appointment. Tests followed, and then anxious waiting. It was no surprise when the test results came back that the fertility problem lay with me, but it was perhaps the first time I felt a twinge of guilt that I couldn't give Gibs the child we both wanted. There followed a referral to a gynaecologist, a minor gynaecological procedure and then a course of Clomid (a fertility drug) to boost my ovulation. Hope surged, but it was thwarted again month after month. Another sadness was the gynaecologist's admission that if I had been referred to him sooner, he might have been able to help us more.

Family culture

Despite the fact that our extended family in the Solomon Islands knew that we really wanted a child and that they were praying for us, I was astounded when a letter arrived from Sister Esther:

Dearest Brother Gibson and Sister-in-law Sally,

Greetings in the name of our Lord Jesus Christ. My husband Ruel and I would like you to adopt our third son Grayven. We know that you formed a special bond with him, Sally, when you were visiting us here, and Grayven would like to be your son. He told us, "If Uncle Gibs and Auntie Sally can't have children, why can't I be their boy?"

Please write to tell us if you would accept him as your son.

Our love in Christ as always,

Sister Esther and Brother-in-law Ruel

This blew my mind and was beyond my understanding; why would they be willing to give up one of their children?

"It's because they love him, Sally, and they believe that he would get better opportunities being brought up in England," Gibs explained to me. So, my disbelief turned to joy – perhaps God was answering our prayers in a different way to what we expected.

So, we started to make plans. Our friend Ken, who was a fellow volunteer with me and one of Gibs' best men at our wedding, had returned to the Solomon Islands to continue his work as a solicitor. We e-mailed him: "Ken, please can you help us? Gibs' sister has offered for us to adopt one of their sons, Grayven, please can you look into the process of how we can bring him back to England." In line with this, we made arrangements to go to spend Christmas 2004 with the family in the Solomon Islands, with the plan of bringing Grayven home with us. Much to our delight, our dear friends, John and Barbara (Mum Barbara and Dad John to us) asked to come with us. They were the first English visitors we ever took to the Solomon Islands, and theirs' is another story of God's wonderful provision, but that is not my story to tell here.

We checked in at Heathrow Airport, went through security, and I suggested a leisurely meal before our first long flight. However, somehow I lost track of time, and an announcement of the last call for our flight saw us running the distance to the boarding gate – not a good reflection on the organisational skills I pride myself on, but it has given us plenty to laugh about since. The few days spent sightseeing in Brisbane were an adventure in all senses of the word, including holding koala bears, and the restaurant meal when Gibs tried kangaroo meat. The four of us continued on our journey to Honiara, where Gibs and I met up with Ken. He had been working on our behalf, and told us, "I have arranged a meeting for you with the Deputy High Commissioner, Gibs and Sally, as you need to talk about getting Grayven into school on your return to England."

This turned out to be a really sad meeting. The Deputy High Commissioner spoke to us kindly, sensing our certain disappointment: "It is not possible for you to take Grayven back home to England with you. England does not recognise the Solomon Islands' adoption process, and children cannot be taken into England for adoption unless there has been parental death or family breakdown. As neither of these circumstances are the case, I am sorry, but your plans cannot go ahead." Our hopes were dashed. Plus, on reaching Gibs' village a few days later, we had to explain this to a sad little boy, who had thought he would be returning to England with us. In reflection, I realise that I went through a grieving process – it felt as if we had lost a child.

A way forward

Adoption had always been an option at the back of my mind, but in Gibs' culture, it happened automatically, when for some reason a child needed to be brought up by the extended family. Therefore, you can imagine my surprise, when almost a year after the disappointment of not being able to adopt Grayven, Gibs said to me "I think we should try to adopt in England."

I remember the conversation vividly. We were on holiday in Turkey, walking back to our hotel after going out for an evening meal. My first reaction was, "I might be too old now," as I was already 49 years old. However, it was the green light I needed, and when we returned home, I didn't waste any time in looking into it.

Christmas week of 2005 heralded our first visit from an adoption social worker. To our surprise, the initial questions posed were not about my age (perhaps helped by the fact that Gibs is a lot younger than me), but about whether we were smokers and whether we were overweight. Fortunately, we didn't fall into either of those categories. This first visit began a long and arduous process, where we felt that we were turned inside out, upside down, and round about, as every area of our lives was examined in great depth. All I can say is that it's a good job it's not a mandatory process you must go through before conceiving your own child, or I believe the human race would be extinct by now! We did think that our lives were too simple to be believed, as neither of us had previous serious relationships, or already had children. There were times in the process when the emotional toll was so great, that we questioned whether to go on, but in the spring of 2006, we attended adoption training, and we felt we were truly on the road forward. However, the process was about to come to an abrupt halt.

A big hiccup?

In June 2006, a letter arrived from Dewsbury Hospital inviting me to go for my first ever mammogram. As I am sure many ladies would agree, not a pleasant procedure (especially when you are not well-endowed in that region!), but a necessary one. It was just a routine medical procedure, so I thought, until I was recalled for a biopsy. The result came through, and I was in total shock, as like a random bomb dropping from the sky, I was suddenly landed with a diagnosis of breast cancer. My first somewhat irrational reaction to the news was, "Now they won't let us adopt." Indeed, the whole process was paused, and it was as if we were suspended in mid air. But the God who promises never to fail or forsake his children (Hebrews 13:5), did not abandon us. After a successful operation and a miraculously speedy recovery, the adoption team agreed to continue working with us. The visits were reduced to fortnightly, but the necessary information continued to be gathered.

A new nest

Our home in Batley had suited our needs as a couple, but with the process going forward we were planning to become a family, so we needed something more – preferably with a garden and play space. In addition to this, we felt a prompting of God to move to Leeds, so we put our house on the market in September 2006. It was another long, slow process. Someone once said, "Never pray for patience, as God will find ways of giving it to you!" We eventually got a buyer in February 2007, but the sale wasn't completed until April and we finally moved in May. We had bid for one house in South Leeds, but someone beat us to it. In the long term, we were grateful, as we ended up buying the house opposite, which had a decent sized garden and backed onto a field. Kind Christian friends helped us settle in, and one couple gave us a sizeable gift to get the work that was needed on the house done. Practically, we were all set for increase.

Parallel action

Alongside all the business of putting a house on the market, the adoption vetting was continuing. The social worker made visits to our referees, who vouched for us, and police checks were made. Then came the next hitch. Despite the fact that Gibs had been in England for more than five years and was included in the police checks here, they decided that he needed to be checked in the Solomon Islands. The only way to do this was to send his fingerprints out there, so they could check them against their records. This was duly done, and in time the response came back – happily, he had a clear record!

The focus moved onto what we wanted our family to look like. This is a strange thing to consider, as we know that in the natural you don't get to choose, but it is an important part of the adoption process. It is a wonderful gift to be able to tell your adopted children that they are special because you chose them, and perhaps it counteracts some of their feelings of rejection that they were 'given away' by their birth parents. We gave time to discussing our dreams of a family, and there were things we were both agreed on: we wanted more than one child, and we didn't want to go through the gruelling assessment process all over again; like many other couples we wanted a child to be as young as possible when he or she came to be part of our family; and we did not feel we had the capacity to take on a child with disabilities. In addition to this, I knew that Gibs would really like a boy – perhaps for a man it is the importance of carrying on the family line.

In June 2007, a month after we moved house, and eighteen months after that initial adoption social worker visit, we went before the adoption panel. It was an emotionally charged experience, sitting before a group of professionals and an adoptive parent, being assessed to see if we could be suitable parents – somewhat bizarre, as again, this is not something anyone has to go through to be natural parents! The most probing questions related to our faith. "What will you do if your children don't want to follow your faith? What will you do if your children are homosexual?" They were questioning our core values, but it gave us an opportunity to explain the essence of our faith. There was no hesitation as I boldly told them, "God's love is unconditional and we will seek to give our children this unconditional love no matter what the circumstances." The verdict followed, and what triumph and great joy filled our hearts, as we were recommended to go forward as adoptive parents.

So it was, that in our new nest, we met our family finder social worker, Annice. She was a lovely lady and soon felt like a family friend. In early July she told us of a baby boy, Peter, who was up for adoption. She told us that Peter's birth Mum was expecting her second child and it was unlikely that she would be allowed to keep the second baby, so it would fulfil our desire to adopt more than one child. When she showed us a photo, we were hooked, we had fallen in love. In August 2007, we went to the Matching Panel.

The decision

If you had been there, you would have felt the tension in the air. We were sitting in the waiting room; I was nervously massaging Gibs' hand as we waited for the verdict. Then the door opened and Annice, our family finder, came in (I swear she had sprouted a halo and wings), "Good News! They have agreed the placement. Peter is going to be your son." We had come to the end of five years of trying for a baby, and 21 months going through the adoption process. This was the answer we had been waiting for, this was a new beginning for us as a family, and at 51 years old I was going to be a Mummy at last, and Gibs' was going to have his dream of being a Daddy.

Peter's placement was agreed in the August. There was a whirlwind of excited preparations and introductions, and by the October he was at home with us, BUT he wasn't legally ours and a future date was set for the adoption court hearing. We thought it was just a formality, until we were told that the birth mother could turn up at the court in the morning to appeal the decision. Well the day came, and the adoption order went through, and best of all, Peter was given a new birth certificate in our name – Peter Solomon.

Growing family

In December 2007 Peter's bother, Joe, was born, but the birth parents had moved to Blackpool, so we did not hear the news until January 2008. Even though we had already stated that we would like to adopt Peter's sibling, the process to release him for adoption had to be gone through all over again. The positive news was that the birth Mum said that if she couldn't keep her second child, she wanted him to go to be with his brother. So in December 2008 we went to meet Joe for the first time in his foster home, and in January 2009, our friends John and Barbara came with us to Blackpool for a week to help look after Peter whilst we had visits with Joe. It was a busy week, but at the end of it we came home as a family of four, and so the fun began!

Chapter 11

"In Sickness And In Health"

The "C" word

The year is 2006 and I am sitting in a sterile hospital waiting room. My friend Julie is by my side, as Gibs had to be at work. As I look around at the people, they are each caught up in their inner world, for many of them this waiting is paralysing their future through fear. If you had been there, you might have heard my heart pounding with nervous anticipation. A nurse calls my name, "Sally Ben," and I am trying to read the expression on her face. We follow her into the small claustrophobic room, where the consultant is studying my notes, rather too intently. Then the words nobody wants to hear echo into the hollow room, "It is cancer." I burst into tears and blurt out, "Now they won't let us adopt." The medics are quick to assure me that the cancer is breast threatening, rather than life threatening, but you can see that my priorities lay elsewhere.

It was a roller coaster period leading up to this appointment. The letter had come inviting me to go for a mammogram. I made the appointment and then protested when I attended that I wasn't yet fifty. The response was that they called ladies before their 50th birthday, when they were carrying out the service in the area. Then came the second letter, advising me that I needed to return to have an irregularity checked out. At this return appointment, they do a procedure to remove some of the tissue for testing. Even though there was no history of breast cancer in my family, somewhere deep within me, I knew what the result was going to be. Again, the Holy Spirit's warning of something that is to come.

When the darkness closes in

We were singing a song in church at the time, "Blessed be your name." I can remember one Sunday morning standing singing resolutely, holding back the tears:

Every blessing you pour out, I'll turn back to praise
When the darkness closes in Lord, still I will say
Blessed be the name of the Lord, blessed be Your name
Blessed be the name of the Lord, blessed be your glorious
name

I knew that my Lord had promised to sustain me and there is never a circumstance in which we should not praise him, even when we don't understand what is happening.

After the diagnosis appointment, Julie took me back to her house. The three of us – Julie, her husband Ian (my church Pastor), and myself – stood embracing each other, and we prayed. One of the hardest tasks came next. I rang my Mum, who lived 250 miles away, to tell her the news. Strangely, I felt guilty inflicting this anxiety on her, as if it was my fault. My Mum was understandably upset, and my faithful friend Julie promised to ring her later to check she was OK.

Gibs came home from work that afternoon and I shared the news with him. I am forever grateful for this wonderful man of God. We talked, we cried, we prayed.

During the evening I received a well-meaning telephone call from a relative who had medical knowledge, but it left me feeling drained. So we booked to go away at the weekend, to a lovely apartment in Slaithwaite, Yorkshire. I was battling with lots of questions. Was it the sun bed treatments I had indulged in during my twenties that had caused this? Or could it be the fertility treatment I had taken to try to conceive? Was this to be the end of my time on earth? Had God's purpose for me been to bring Gibs to England and now he was ready to take me home? Gibs and I took this time to talk and share together, as we do everything in our lives, and we found strength together for the battle ahead.

The operation

The National Health Service (NHS) was quick to move once I had received the diagnosis. We were called to a hospital, where we met with a consultant. He told us that the only possible treatment was a single mastectomy. However, we had to make a decision as to whether I would have an immediate implant after the mastectomy, or a prosthetic breast. It was too much for me to take in, but Gibs, standing by my side, helped me make the decision. The mastectomy followed by the immediate implant it would be. I was still shocked when the operation date came through for a fortnight later. Did the urgency mean it was really a matter of life and death? But after a discussion with the consultant, we were able to delay it for another couple of weeks, as my Aunt and Uncle who lived in Canada were in England and planning to visit us over the first operation date. They were a wonderful Christian couple and it was really important to me to spend some time with them. Sometimes your mental health is as important as your physical health.

Gibs had been learning to drive for some months. He had mastered the skills, despite the fact that driving was not commonplace in the Solomon Islands when Gibs grew up there. However, after numerous attempts, passing the practical test was still eluding him. Now the crunch came. The hospital where my operation was to take place was several miles away and not easily accessible by public transport. He had another test booked in for the week before my operation. He told his driving instructor, "I have to pass this time, as I need to be able to visit my wife in hospital, and she won't be allowed to drive for a few weeks after the operation." God hears our cries! Imagine our elation, when he called me to say, "I passed!"

The night before the operation, the consultant visited me on the ward. I could not feel the lump, and I was bold enough to tell him that I believed in a God who heals and perhaps he had healed me. He brushed this aside, and I woke up in the morning to the "Nil by mouth" sign in preparation for the operation. It is often harder to be the one watching the one you love go through the trial. Gibs told me later that he spent the morning flat on his face crying before God, asking him why I had to go through this. But the mastectomy and the implant went ahead, and when I came round from the anaesthetic, I was hooked up to the drip providing pain relief.

Sometimes God delivers a miracle immediately through prayer, and at other times he delivers it in other ways, such as through medical professionals. Sceptics would say that I was just fortunate, but I know that my God delivered my miracle through a series of events. The first being that when dear friends John and Barbara visited in the evening after my operation, Barbara said that I looked better than I had in a long time – perhaps it was the rest that did it! Then I started doing the recommended exercises the following day, much to the amazement of the physiotherapist, and I was discharged after only two nights, not the usual five nights.

The following two weeks were an anxious wait to hear the test results, as to whether any cancerous cells had been found in the lymph nodes. The appointment came through, and not only were the lymph nodes clear, but I didn't have to take any medication or have any follow up treatment – a tremendous blessing, as naturally your mind plays with the possibility of chemotherapy, etc. Julie had told us to book a holiday for when this was over. So the completion of our miracle came, when six weeks after the operation, it was us this time visiting my Aunt and Uncle in Canada, and amazingly I was recovered enough to paddle a kayak on a lake in Vancouver!

Time can be a strange phenomenon. Despite the fact that I bear the scar in my body, as the years have passed, it has felt unreal, as if I was speaking of somebody else having breast cancer. However, there can be purpose in everything, and I am grateful for the opportunities I have had to come alongside other ladies diagnosed with breast cancer. I am sure my psychological healing has also been helped by my husband, who still tells me my body is beautiful (this could be affected by his condition that I am going to tell you about in the next section!). I am also grateful that I have not struggled with fears of developing cancer in my other breast, but time also dulled the memory of the consultant telling me, "Breast implants last for ten - fifteen years." Hence in 2020, in the middle of the COVID-19 crisis, an online consultation sent me back to the hospital, where it was confirmed that the implant has ruptured and further surgery will be required. Thankfully this isn't urgent, and as our wonderful NHS service tries to cope in the aftermath of the pandemic, I am still on the waiting list, but back to the hospital I will go!

For now we see in a mirror darkly

Fast forward now to the end of December 2016, Gibs has returned from a holiday in the Solomon Islands with Peter. "Sally, my eyes really troubled me in the bright sunlight at home. It was like I was looking through a mist all the time. I even got two of my sisters mixed up!" We arranged a routine eye test appointment, I thought he might need glasses. However, at the appointment he was diagnosed with cataracts and referred to the hospital for further investigations. We attended the hospital appointment together, totally unprepared for the outcome. Thorough tests were conducted and the consultant examined his eyes, before asking a series of questions: "When did you first notice this cloudiness with your vision? Do you have any problems with your hearing? Does anyone in your family suffer with sight loss or hearing loss?" It is strange how when changes happen over time, you don't always identify them. The answers to the questions made us realise that his difficulties were not entirely new, he had previously had problems distinguishing shades of light, and he did have some hearing loss as well. The consultant explained to us, "I am sorry to tell you that the tests and examinations reveal something much more debilitating than cataracts. You have a genetic disorder, that will eventually lead to blindness, and also causes hearing loss."

We were back on the emotional roller coaster, this time with me sitting in the passenger seat. The consultant had continued, striking the final blow, "Do you drive, Gibson?" When Gibs answered that he did, the consultant carried on, "Then you must have a test to check your field of vision to see if it it safe for you to continue to drive." Obediently, Gibs undertook the test, and you can imagine the blow to his morale, when a negative result came back. He was devastated, I think it is one of the lowest points I have seen him at in our life together. He had to relinquish his driving licence and, after ten years of driving in Britain, he felt that he lost some of his independence.

Keep asking, keep knocking

Currently, there is no cure or treatment for his condition, which has been named as Usher's disease. I pray for his eyes and ears every night before we sleep, and of course many others have prayed for him, but we still wait for our miracle. What we do know is that God has told us to declare his faithfulness in the midst of our circumstances. Gibs himself really relates to St Paul's words in 2 Corinthians 12:7-9: "I was given a thorn in my flesh, a messenger of Satan, to torment me. Three times I pleaded with the Lord to take it away from me. But he said to me, 'My grace is sufficient for you, for my power is made perfect in weakness.' Therefore I will boast all the more gladly about my weaknesses, so that Christ's power may rest on me." Some Bible commentators believe that St Paul's 'thorn in the flesh' was also a problem with his eyes, so I suppose Gibs is in good company with one of the leading apostles!

We make life adjustments accordingly. I naturally guide Gibs when we come to steps, and there are greater limitations on what he can do with the boys. Just as I have to deal with the guilt that can still come up, of not being able to give Gibs' a birth child, he has to deal with the guilt he feels that all of the ferrying around of the boys now lands on me. However, there are blessings, like a disabled parking pass, and a free bus pass! Plus, at times, it brings compassion out of the boys, which is delightful to see. On one occasion Gibs was worshipping with his guitar, crying out to God for his eyesight. Joe came into the room, "What's wrong Daddy?"

"I am feeling sad, Joe, that I can't see properly, and I am asking God to help me. Could you pray for me?"

Joe responded, "Please, Jesus, make Daddy's eyes better." Then he held up fingers in front of Gibs face and asked him how many he could see. When Gibs answered correctly, Joe said, "It's OK Daddy, you can see!"

Hope

To my shame, I admit that I never took much interest in medical research, until it affected us. At Gibs' annual review appointment, the consultant explained to us: "Genetic testing has established that you have three faulty genes, Gibson. Research is currently underway to try to come up with a treatment for Usher's disease. To know if this treatment would be suitable for you, we have to establish which of your faulty genes is causing the disease in your body. To do this, we need to give your brother and sisters a genetic test, to identify the rogue gene." Sounds sensible, except that his brother and sisters are in the Solomon Islands, 9,147 miles away from the UK! The plan was to send kits out to the Solomons with someone travelling there, and for them to be posted back to the hospital. It didn't work out! So we are now in 2021, waiting for the lifting of the global pandemic restrictions, so that we can visit and take the tests out with us ourselves.

"Look at this Sally, there is a private clinic in Berlin that offers treatment for Retinitis Pigmentosa (the visual part of Usher's disease)", Gibs announced to me excitedly in 2019.

"Where have you found that, Gibs?"

"I googled it and there are posts on Facebook from people who have benefitted from the treatment." Miss Cautious here was sceptical.

"If it is a bonafide treatment, why don't the consultants here know about it?" But he was so enthusiastic, we had to pursue it. We contacted the clinic in Berlin and the consultant in Leeds. The consultant in Leeds was so helpful, providing test results that the doctor in Berlin required, and assuring us that if we wanted to try the treatment, it shouldn't harm Gibs' vision further, even if it didn't provide an improvement.

The doctor at the clinic examined the English test results and confirmed that they could offer Gibs treatment. My mind went again to the thought of my Dad smiling down on us – thanks to the inheritance he left us, we could finance the trip. Our heavenly Dad was smiling down on us, too – a German friend whom we had met at Pacific gatherings offered for us to stay with him in his flat in Berlin. However, we needed another miracle – who would look after our boys? God's arm is never too short.

Mandy, another Pacific friend, who lives in Cornwall, rang Gibs one morning to tell him about the death of her brother in Australia. As the conversation progressed, she asked, "How are your eyes, Gibs?" Gibs explained about the possibility of treatment in Berlin, but said we had no one to stay with the boys. Mandy's quick response was: "I have taken early retirement. I will come up with my grandson, who is in his twenties, and stay with the boys!" We were all systems go.

So the end of September 2019 found Gibs and I in Berlin. The treatment consisted of electrical stimulation therapy, and trained the brain to use cells that had become dormant. Most days we spent a few hours at the clinic, but we were also able to explore Berlin, which was fascinating. The highlight of the whole trip was a moment in the Natural History Museum. Gibs and I had become separated by a short distance and I was off to one side of him, but he saw me wave to him. Then he said, "Something has changed. Before, in a place like this, people were on top of me before I saw them, but today I have space around me." We were elated.

On our return to England, he reported another improvement that he could read the neon signs in the bus shelters. However, there was no change to the mistiness that continually clouds his eyes. I was frustrated and felt I had failed him, when I made an unsuccessful attempt to purchase a touch screen so that he could continue with the exercises that he had done at the clinic. Nevertheless, we had grasped the opportunity offered to us, and there was hope.

No end yet

The latest check-up shows that there has not been any further deterioration to his sight, for which we are grateful, but the mistiness has not cleared. So there is no end yet to this particular part of our story. Who knows if our God of miracles will step in and heal him for his glory? It would certainly be a testimony to many who know of his condition, but our testimony is that God is faithful, no matter what the path we walk.

Sally and Gibs at the Brandenburg Gate

Chapter 12

To the Ends of The Earth

"But you will receive power when the Holy Spirit comes on you; and you will be my witnesses in Jerusalem, and in all Judea and Samaria, and to the ends of the earth." (Acts 1:8)

This was the promise of Jesus after his resurrection in the days before he ascended back to heaven. In the Solomon Islands, they believe that the Christian gospel coming to their land was when it reached the ends of the earth.

The South Seas Evangelical Mission

Blackbirding was the practice in the late 1800s of enslaving South Pacific Islanders on the cotton and sugar plantations of Queensland, Australia. These slaves were known as Kanakas. One of the Islanders was Peter Ambuofa from Malaita Province (Gibs' Island), and he was converted to Christianity whilst working on the plantations. In 1894 he returned to Malaita to share the gospel with his people. To begin with, his relatives shunned him, but as they witnessed miracles in his life, they too became Christians. In 1904 Peter asked for help from the Queensland Kanaka Mission, and a lady called Florence Young brought a party of missionaries to Malaita. This eventually led to the creation of the South Seas Evangelical Mission, which is the church Gibs was a member of in the Solomon Islands.

To the ears of the western volunteers, it was strange to hear Christian music blasting out of the cafe stalls, but it was reflective of the Solomon Islands' strong Christian tradition. To me, it was a great joy to marry into a family who lived by their Christian faith. When we returned to the Solomon Islands for a visit at the end of 2000, we had a wonderful Island celebration of our marriage, complete with a local panpipe band and traditional dancers. We were also prayed for in the local church: "Gibson, we commission you as a missionary to England. The gospel was brought to the Solomon Islands, now it is time for it to be taken back to England." Many no longer class England as a Christian country, and Gibs certainly had much to teach us from his culture and his walk with God.

The international ministry

"Ask me, and I will make the nations your inheritance, the ends of the earth your possession." (Psalm 2:8)

Having overcome his fear of going out into the streets of Dewsbury, Gibs found himself to be not just the only black face, but also the only international person in our church. Our Christian belief is that the church is not the building, but the believers that you fellowship with, and you are joined in God's family with these believers. Family relationships can be a challenge, but how much more so when you perceive yourself as the outsider? The church members embraced him, and we tried to fit in with a small group, but we both had a desire to reach out to people from other nations and draw them into the family of God.

We sat down with our Pastors, Ian and Julie, and shared our hearts:

"Each of us has felt that we want to help people of different nationalities. We have talked about this together and feel that my experience of living in Gibs' country, and his experience of adjusting to living in England, have set us up to do this."

"We think it's a great idea, how would you go about it?" was their enthusiastic response.

"We would like to invite people into our home. Sharing a meal is something that crosses all cultures, and our home is where we can make them feel most welcome."

Our Pastors happily gave us the green light, but how could we get started? Well, you may have gathered in reading our story this far, that we believe that when God gives you an idea, he also gives you a way to work it out.

106

We read in a local newspaper that a group of Filipino nurses had come to Dewsbury to work in the local hospital, but they were not being treated well. Being the organiser in our marriage partnership, I wrote a letter to the head of nursing, explaining who we were, and asking her to give them an invitation to come and have a meal at our home. There was no response. We learnt later that the head of nursing had advised them to refuse this invitation, as they didn't know anything about us and she was concerned for their welfare.

However, God was on the case, and we found the address of a house where six of them were living (I won't tell you how, in these days of data privacy!). One day, very boldly, I went and knocked on the door. Rowena, who became one of our dearest friends, opened the door.

"I am the lady, along with my husband who is from another country, who wrote to the head of nursing to invite you all to come to our house for a meal."

Rowena smiled warmly and took my phone number, promising to talk to the others about a suitable date. She told us later, that she was reminded of the Bible verse "Show hospitality to strangers, for they may be angels from God showing up as your guests." (Hebrews 13:2) True to her word, she contacted us, and she came with another lady, Joy, to eat at our home. So began the international ministry.

Rowena's story was like others' we have heard over the years: "I was working as a nurse in the Philippines, but I couldn't make enough money to feed my family. An opportunity arose to come and work in England, so I applied and I was successful. I had to leave my husband and my four boys behind, it nearly broke my heart, as our youngest son is only four years old, but I couldn't let them starve." We first met Rowena in March 2001 and imagine our joy, when in August 2001 we were able to help her to bring her husband and four boys over to England to join her. We became Auntie Sally and Uncle Gibs, and our international family grew.

Many of our new-found Filipino friends had a strong Catholic background, but they did not enjoy a personal relationship with the Lord Jesus Christ as we do. Joy, our other first time visitor alongside Rowena, started dating Emil, another of the Filipinos. One evening he called us: "You know that I share a house with some of the other Filipino nurses. People have reported seeing someone at the window, when none of us were in. We are scared, please can you come and pray in the house?"

We duly went round to the house and Gibs prayed in each room of the house. However, Emil was unable to accompany us around the house as he had a very swollen knee.

"May I pray for your knee as well?" Gibs asked Emil.

"Sure, it can't make it any worse," Emil replied with a shy smile. Then, "Wow, I can feel heat going through my knee!" By the following day, the swelling had gone, and in the days to come there were no further reports of a "ghostly presence" in the house. Emil became a Christian, joined the church, and married Joy!

Over the months and years, our contacts grew and there were more interesting encounters. In 2005, I recorded that 142 people from 26 different countries visited our international group or the church. We bought an eight-seater people carrier, as new international friends needed transport to come to church. We thanked God for the SatNav as we found our way around the streets of Dewsbury and Batley. Our black/white combination proved powerful. We had made contact with a young African gentleman and we went to pick him up one Sunday. A fellow housemate opened the door and disappeared upstairs. We heard some negotiation take place before he joined us, and later he told us, "I only came with you because Gibs is black and you are white."

We had much to learn of different cultures and customs, but this international diversity was bringing richness to the church as the numbers of international members grew over the years.

There were many fun times together, celebrations and International Evenings, where there would be songs and dancing from different nations, and the mandatory food dishes, tastes of the world. The Dewsbury Reporter included a piece on one of these International Evenings:

'The World on a Plate'

More than 100 people from 17 different nations attended an international 'Tastes of the World' evening at New Horizons Church, Dewsbury, on Saturday. Live music was provided by musicians from different parts of the world including Brazilian Claudio Kron who performed a series of percussion pieces, a poetry reading from the Philippines, and dancing from the Solomon Islands and Brazil.

There were masses of food and drink with ingredients used by cooks from various countries. Organisers are hoping to hold other similar events. For more information, contact Sally or Gibson Ben on 01924 488426.

Travel

In February 2001 we took a delayed honeymoon to Tunisia. It was the first country either of us had been to where you are constantly pestered to buy things as you walk along the streets. The vendors try all the common languages to try to persuade you to buy their wares. We devised a strategy. "Gibs, you speak to me in your language all the time we are in earshot and I will answer every time with the few words of your language that I know, 'Naku liothau ani oe (I love you)'." This worked, as the vendors could not identify the language and gave up on us. They didn't know that I hadn't a clue what Gibs was saying to me!

In 2002, our destination was Colombia in South America. We went as part of a small group from our church to an international Christian conference, which was attended by thousands of people from many nations. At that time the safety of tourists was a prime factor, we were advised not to leave our hotel unaccompanied, and armed guards escorted us on and off of the conference buses. The conference meetings themselves were amazing, reminiscent of a football stadium full of celebrating spectators, except we were celebrating Jesus Christ our King and Victor in life.

Thinking of his parochial village background, Gibs is totally amazed how his horizons have broadened and that he has now visited six of the seven continents of the world (even if Asia is only included due to an overnight stop-over!). In truth, countries benefit from his presence, as whichever country he visits, he gets a burden to pray for that nation while he is there.

We had opportunities through the church to accompany others on mission trips. Then, we were so excited when the church sent us as a family on a mission trip to Romania. This was an incredible experience, and we felt a foretaste of things to come. Gibs and I both had the opportunity to speak in the church, and our boys had a great time as the young people looked after them and entertained them. Gibs also put his other skills to work, when he painted a sign for the church.

In 2017 we pushed the boat out (financially and by taking the boys out of school for two months) and took an extended trip as a family, testing the waters as to whether our future lay in another country. At the beginning of the trip, we spent time in Cebu in the Philippines, where Rowena's (the Filipino friend at home) family welcomed us like royalty. We then moved on to the Province of Palawan, to connect with a church there and visit the Compassion Project that they ran. Compassion is an organisation that arranges for people in England to sponsor children in developing countries to receive education, health care and life skills. How wonderful it was to join the Saturday sessions and witness the children thriving in their classes. It was very moving too for me to hear Gibs encourage the children: "Make the most of this opportunity you have here. God has amazing things planned for you. I came from a small village far away from here, but God has opened up the whole world to me."

"Hearts of Hope"

From the Philippines we travelled on to the Solomon Islands, where we had offered to volunteer for a charity on Gibs' Island, called 'Hearts Of Hope' (HOH). We had met the HOH president, Janet Aihari, in 2015, when we were holidaying on the Island. The charity's motto is taken from the Bible verse, James 1:27: "Religion that God our Father accepts as pure and faultless is this: to look after orphans and widows in their distress and to keep oneself from being polluted by the world." This same verse had prompted Gibs to give similar help at his village, Onebusu, in north Malaita, when we had been on holiday breaks in 2004, 2006, 2015 and 2016.

Janet, and other volunteers from the charity, met us at the wharf and we were presented with flower garlands. She had arranged for the local reporter to be there and an article appeared in the Solomon Star newspaper the following day. She reflected that HOH had in the past tried its best to improve and strengthen its administration work such as formulating and drafting proposals and projects. The plan was for me to help with administration work, while Gibs would take a lead in village outreach programs, using his language and musical skills.

Janet wanted to give us time to settle in, but eventually, conscious that we had limited time (and the fact that I like action!) we pushed to get going. Friends in England had supported us in fundraising, so one of the first tasks was to go shopping for goods to give the widows and orphans. Janet's team would find out the numbers of orphans and widows in a community, then we would spend time at Janet's house making up parcels.

The outreaches themselves were a humbling experience. What a privilege it was to present gifts to the widows and orphans. In one community, Fa'arau, we presented two gifts to widows in their homes, as they were unable to walk about. The first visit was to a widow, Elsie, who was 106 years old. The dear lady lived in her small leaf house and told us of the miracles of healing God had done in her life. We prayed for her, and she in turn prayed for us. The local school fundraising was taking place and the school committee kindly allowed us to present the gifts to ten more widows and widowers, and 32 orphans before their programme commenced. The gifts consisted of blankets, washing soap, tea leaves, sugar and rice for the widows and widowers, and sheets, washing soap, toothpaste and toothbrush, exercise book, biro and pencil for the orphans. Very basic items in our minds, but necessities for the recipients.

Janet and her husband Adrian supported the charity sacrificially. On this occasion they had harvested twenty pumpkins from their own garden to bless the families in the community. Other children in the community were given Twists (like cheese puff crisps) and lollipops, so as not to miss out on the treats. It was wonderful to see the joy on the faces of those who received the gifts. A spokesman for the community told us that the work of HOH reaches the grass roots of the communities, unlike many other initiatives. He said they were all very grateful for the support of HOH.

We travelled to six community outreaches in total, usually by truck, but on one occasion by motorised canoe. It is remarkable how the canoe driver navigates the way from one location to another with just their knowledge of the seascape. This trip turned into a real adventure, when as evening was falling on the return journey, the motor on the canoe broke down. Would we be stranded for the night? We managed to dock at a village wharf and this was where we learnt of the positive reputation of HOH, when the village committee were willing to lend another motor, so thankfully we did arrive home that night! At every outreach, Gibs would play his guitar and we enjoyed singing together as part of the programmes. Every time we would see the joy of the recipients of the simple gifts, some of the children were shy, but some of the bolder widows would dance up to receive their gifts, delighting us all.

Tastes of the Pacific

For me, marrying Gibs opened up a whole new world. I now had two homes, one in England, and one in the Solomon Islands, and I really felt I was of dual nationality. Gibs' paintings displayed around our home, along with artefacts, such as a wood carving of a war canoe and exotic sea shells, keep the Pacific in our daily lives. In the summer of 2001, Gibs went out to the Solomon Islands to visit his family, then we arranged to meet in Vanuatu for a holiday together, so I had a taste of another Pacific country. Vanuatu was a French colony and so had French influences, rather than the British ones of the Solomon Islands. Images that these tropical islands conjure up, of coconut palms, long sandy beaches and warm seas, are in truth the reality. One of many highlights of the holiday was swimming with a dugong in the sea (a dugong is a mammal similar to a sea cow).

Over the years, we have made contact with other Solomon Islanders and other Pacific Islanders living in England. One of our early contacts was with Bishop Willy, who was the parish priest in Congleton, where he lived with his family. In 2004, Gibs worked with Bishop Willy to plan the first Solomon Islands Independence celebration in England, which Bishop Willy hosted in Congleton. This has become an annual event and most years we have been able to attend, a great time of Island food and entertainment. There have also been other Pacific celebrations, some of which Gibs has been invited to take his paintings to offer for sale. As mentioned in another chapter, we were very excited to travel down to London in 2018, to the gathering to mark the setting up of the Solomon Islands' High Commission (which sadly closed again in 2021 due to the Covid pandemic). Gibs marvelled that he had never met the Solomon Islands' Prime Minister in his own country, but he met him at this event in London.

The nations in our home

How I love introducing international people to the finer English traditions. One Christmas, we had four single people staying with us, all of them far from their native homes. What fun I had in the lead up to Christmas buying stocking fillers, and what excitement there was on Christmas morning, when they were each presented with a Christmas stocking, something they had never experienced. Later in the day, there were eight of us at the Christmas dinner table, representing six nations, and we enjoyed (well I hope they did!) a traditional English Christmas dinner and spent the afternoon playing games.

Another stage of our international journey was having international people to live with us. We first responded to a request for a Swiss young man to be part of a family in England for six months to improve his English – and perhaps it was good practice for us having a teenager in the house! Next, a dear lady from Colombia joined our family for several months, also to improve her English. The most recent additions were two men, one from the Solomon Islands and one from Papua New Guinea. They were doing courses at Leeds University and they asked if they could live with us as they completed their studies in order to be able to save some money. With five males in the house I was definitely outnumbered, but I was treated well. We are still in contact with all of these people and they certainly added to the richness of our family life.

Chapter 13

Family Snapshots

Early days

Walking along the road pushing Peter in his buggy, my heart was singing – I was a mum at last, and I don't think anyone could have been happier. He was a really happy, docile baby, and I thoroughly enjoyed my adoption leave. I talked to him constantly and shared every rhyme and nursery song with him that I had learnt in my early years training. We were regular attendees at the "Stay and Play" sessions at our local children's centre and here we made friends with other parents and their young children. We celebrated all his landmarks, his first steps and his first words, one of which was guitar. This reflected his love for his Daddy, who would play his guitar for him, and Peter began early on with his love of drumming, banging pans with a wooden spoon.

In January 2009, Joe joined our family and we started to celebrate his landmarks as well. Joe was fostered in a single parent family, but he quickly latched onto Gibs as Daddy. After a shorter adoption leave, I went back to work and Gibs became the main carer for both boys, something that will fill any parent of young children with admiration.

One afternoon, Gibs had collected Peter from nursery. He settled him at the table with a drink and a snack whilst he took Joe upstairs to change his nappy, but when he came down, Peter had gone! Gibs was frantic, and even more so when he realised that he had not locked the front door. He set off up the hill to the nursery looking for Peter and alerting neighbours as he went, but Peter was nowhere to be seen. He didn't waste anymore time, he rang 999 (English police emergency number). The police were quickly in attendance, taking the details and a description of Peter, and soon the police helicopter could be heard hovering over the estate where we live. The policeman in attendance then asked to do a routine search of the house. He checked the cupboard in the dining room, nothing, then as he turned around, he said, "Is that him?" Sure enough, Peter had fallen into a deep sleep over his snack and slipped down between his chair and the table, completely out of sight! Panic over, thanks given, and search called off. The first I knew of it was when I picked up my phone messages at the end of my day's work, when fortunately it was just a story for the memories book.

I woke up with a start and was immediately alert. Joe was coughing and gasping for breath. I now knew what that meant, an attack of croup. The first time it happened it was extremely scary, but now we knew what to do. We tried steam in the bathroom, but when that didn't work, I bundled him in the car and set off for A&E (Accident and Emergency), leaving Gibs to look after Peter. Formerly a steroid injection had done the trick, and once it had taken effect we would be on our way home again, but tonight that wasn't so. They wanted him to be kept under observation and allocated him a bed. What none of us were prepared for, was that Joe was feeling better, and as a lively toddler he had other ideas than settling down in a strange bed for the night, despite the late hour! So it was a sleep short night for Mum, no matter that she had work the next day.

In 2008, before Peter was two, and therefore did not need his own seat on the planes, we took him to visit Gibs' family in the Solomon Islands. Then in 2010, as I was working, and Peter had started school, we arranged for Gibs to take Joe to the Solomon Islands on his own. However, they nearly didn't even manage to leave England. At security at Heathrow airport, the officer questioned him suspiciously: "Is this your son?"

"Yes, he is."

"Where are you going?"

"I'm taking him to my country, the Solomon Islands, to meet my family."

"Please wait here whilst I speak to a senior officer."

For Gibs this was deja vu from when he had first arrived in England and we were detained by the immigration officers, questioning the legitimacy of our pending marriage and his right to be in England. However, it was Joe who saved the day. By the time the two officers appeared, he was becoming very impatient, and calling out, "Daddy, come on Daddy, we need to go."

"Out of the mouths of babes" comes to mind, as this was proof enough for the officers that Joe really was Gibs' son. On hearing the story, it indicated to me how much we thought of ourselves as a family, as in our naivety, it had not occurred to us that there might be questions about a black man taking a white child out of the country without his mother.

Magic moments

"Record the magic moments," the adoption social worker advised, and I am so glad he did. So before we move onto the tougher stuff in the next chapter (much of which came with the onset of the teenage years), I am going to share with you some of my journal entries, which I hope you will enjoy.

December 2009: I was trying to use the DVD player at my Mum and Dad's, and a scene came on the TV from 'Allo 'Allo! (English TV comedy series). The maid was trying to come into the bedroom, where the man was in bed. She comes in and jumps on top of him in bed. I quickly changed the channel and Peter said, "Naughty lady Mummy, shoes on bed!"

19 April 2010: On Saturday we had dropped Gibs in Dewsbury. The boys asked what he was doing and I told them he had gone to pray for sick people for Jesus to make them better. On Monday, Peter and I saw a dead bird on the beach. I told Peter it was a poor dead bird and he said, "Daddy ask Jesus to make it better!"

7 November 2010: Peter (four years two months), "Where is Jesus Mummy?"

"He can live in your heart and be your friend if you ask him."

"Yes please."

So I prayed and he repeated after me, "Dear Lord Jesus, please come and live in my heart, and be my friend forever."

24 November 2010: Gibs had taken Joe to the Doctors as he had suffered from diarrhoea since he returned from the Solomon Islands. The doctor said he should have 48 hours on clear fluids. As Joe went in he said, "I've got a poorly tummy." As he left he said, "Can I have a biscuit, Doctor?" (The doctor gave children a biscuit when they were good at the surgery!)

1 April 2011: Peter (four years seven months) learnt to ride his two-wheeler bike tonight without stabilisers. It was amazing to watch. After a few times of Daddy holding the saddle, he began to get his balance and eventually was riding long distances across the field!

24 April 2011: We were sitting at the breakfast table talking about what Jesus did for us at Easter. Peter says, "Jesus came back to life again and he lives in my heart."

"Jesus lives in my heart too?" asks Joe (three years five months)

"Not yet, but would you like to ask him to?"

"Yes," and he also repeated a simple prayer after me.

16 July 2011: Joe (three years seven months) rode his two-wheeler bike without stabilisers across the field at the back of our house (copying big brother).

1 March 2012: We could not find Peter's Spiderman hood. Peter told me to ask Jesus where it was, then he said, "Where did he tell you?" – He obviously thought I had a hotline to God! I can't even remember where it turned up, but we certainly thanked Jesus when it did!

10 June 2012: We were driving along in the car and the boys were talking about car colours. Joe said, "I like indigo." I asked him where he learned that word and he said, "It's a song in my head." Then he added, "It's dark purple."

January 2013: Joe told us he wanted to go to see his cousins in the Solomon Islands. We told him it cost lots of money. He said he was going to work hard at school so he could go and see his cousins. He said when the others were playing at school, he would get his learning pack out and do his numbers, his reading, and his writing!

February 2013: I told Joe that his friend was not at school because he had chicken pox. Joe said "No Mummy, his chicken pox have been deleted."

April 2013: We were in a caravan on holiday. The TV lost its signal and Joe asked Jesus to make it right again. When it came right again he said, "I asked Jesus to make it right." We all snuggled up and he said, "Let's be family. This is the best holiday ever."

1 December 2013: I had told Peter that Gibs went to Cottingley Craft Fair to earn some money. Peter said, "I have some money in my money box you can have, Daddy."
Joe retorted, "You can't have the 10p I got for my tooth."

23 September 2014: I had asked Peter to say goodbye to Daddy in the mornings, because Daddy thought Peter didn't miss him. That evening Peter wrote a note for Gibs: "Daddy I'll always be with you when I go to school."

3 February 2015: Gibs and I were going to Poland for a couple of days to celebrate Gibs' 40th. As we were leaving, Joe said to Gibs, "Please, Daddy, can you take a photo of where you stay so you can show me when you get back?" Then he said to me, "I'll miss you Mummy." I told him I'd miss him too, but it was only two days. Then I said, "I love you to the moon and back." He said, "Do you love me to the planets?"

4 March 2015: Peter told the football coach at Cockburn that he had a pain in his side. The coach said, "Have you got a stitch?" Peter replied, "I've never had stitches!"

9 November 2015: Gibs made bows and arrows with the boys. Joe said, "Daddy's a Master."

13 December 2015: Joe had been really cross and rude. I asked him why? He said, "My brain tells me to say it and my heart tells me not to."

27 February 2016: An exciting evening! Gibs had recorded an album of his songs and tonight he did a concert to launch it, sixty people attended. Incredibly, Peter agreed to play the drums (alongside his drum teacher) for one of the songs. He did a great job, and we were so proud of him. What a huge step forward for the boy who wouldn't even collect a certificate in a school assembly.

1 June 2016: Joe had a day out today with Grandma Barbara and Grandad John. He said, "I have enjoyed it this afternoon and life is about enjoying yourself."

24 June 2016: Gibs went to Peter's sports afternoon. They did the three-legged race together, and they won. Then Peter told Gibs, "You are strong Daddy, come and do the tug-of-war." Their team won. Both Peter and Gibs were really excited!

28 June 2016: Peter had a bad case of diarrhoea and had to stay off school. Our financial adviser came to see me, and Peter made his cup of tea. He brought it to the lounge and I asked him if he had brought mine. He said, "I've made it for the guest!"

30 September 2016: Our Filipino friends were having a Thanksgiving Night and they asked Gibs to go and play his guitar and sing. There was a drum kit on the stage, and to our amazement, Peter agreed to accompany Gibs. Perhaps even more amazing, was when he came up to me after playing and said, "I am not shy now Mummy. I have faced my fears!" Where has this son of ours suddenly found the power to express his emotions?

9 December 2016: Gibs and Peter are away in the Solomon Islands. I asked Joe to pray for me as I needed to go to the doctors. He said he didn't know what to pray, so I told him just to ask Jesus to make me better. He prayed, "Please Jesus make Mummy better, and be with Daddy and Peter in the Solomon Islands."

18 June 2017: We are staying in a rented house in Auki on our trip to the Solomon Islands. The next door neighbour gave Peter a duckling. He was delighted.

30 June 2017: Joe was with me in Auki, whilst Gibs was in his village with Peter. Joe was feeling left out, so he mopped up, washed shoes, and tidied our bedroom. Then he put my fan open on my pillow. Melted my heart!

7 July 2017: Our niece, Michelle, got married today in Gibs' village. Both boys, dressed in black trousers, white shirts and waistcoats, stood up with the wedding couple. They did really well and we were so proud.

15 July 2017: Lulu invited Joe to spend the day with her son Simon in the Low Price Store in Auki. They had great fun jumping off the towers of 10kg flour sacks, in between playing on their phones!

10 August 2017: I went to pick Joe up from Yorkshire Camps (a camp run by Christians in the Yorkshire Dales for children and young people). Joe had told the camp leader that he was excited to go home, as he missed the special prayer we said for him each night.

8 November 2017: Joe announced, "Daddy's best at making noodles. And Auntie Esther (Gibs' sister in the Solomon Islands). It must run in the family."

20 January 2018: Peter said to Grandad John, "You're not my real grandad. Don't be offended. My real grandad died, so you are my grandad now."

14 March 2018: Text from school – "Hi Sally, Peter has had a fantastic day and dealt with a disappointment this morning well. He has made a pirate dagger and is bringing it home to show you."

13 April 2018: A report from Yorkshire Camps – "Peter should be proud of himself. Even when he was getting angry, he walked away, thought about it, and calmed himself."

29 May 2018: We had been to a park in the morning and I had warned Joe not to bounce his ball too hard, or he would lose it. Of course, he did just that, and his ball disappeared over the hedge. We searched for it and I asked God to show us where it was, and then I saw it, lodged in the hedge. In the evening we were watching a film where a girl had her prayer answered. I told Joe that we had a miracle this

morning, when God answered my prayer and showed me where his ball was. He said, **"I know the best miracle – that I was adopted into a lovely family."** I write this in bold type, as this is the best gift either of the boys has ever given me and a memory I will treasure forever.

18 June 2018: Joe won a prize at school and chose a new cover for my phone.

4 July 2018: Mr Taylor (music teacher), said he was a "very proud teacher" today, after Peter's Grade One drum exam yesterday.

31 August 2018: I banged my head closing the boot of the car. Joe said, "Are you OK Mummy?" Then, "Please Jesus ..." I prompted, "Please Jesus what?" He responded, "Please Jesus help Mummy's head."

1 September 2018: Peter performed with his band at the end of his first week at School of Rock. I cried tears of joy. I thanked Isaac the leader, and he messaged back: "Thanks Sally – it's been a pleasure working with him this week! So much achieved in such a short time."

8 October 2018: Peter forgot his phone password and he had to pay for it to be unlocked. The man said he would lose everything off his phone, but he didn't. Peter told me, "I prayed that I wouldn't lose it all Mummy."

15 October 2018: Joe managed to get his tablet to charge again and all the apps/games were back – he too said he prayed for it!

23 December 2018: Solomon Island football boys come to stay for Christmas. The three of them were going to stay in Joe's room as the biggest room, but Peter moved his drum kit as he insisted one of them sleep in his room. One of them agreed and at night time Peter asked Gibs to pray for him and also for the footballer.

11 March 2019: Peter's supply teacher e-mailed: "I just want to inform you about Peter's amazing week in school. He has shown great concentration and determination within his work, and has produced some fantastic outcomes. He has also been able to regulate himself and has made some

brilliant choices. He has been a pleasure to teach and has made myself extremely welcome."

8 April 2019: I picked Peter up from School of Rock and the leader told me that Peter had been brilliant and he was really proud of him. There is a blind boy in Peter's group, and Peter had taken him under his wing and befriended him without being asked to.

16 June 2019: A friend, Gary, came with us to church today. In the car we mentioned about going to the Solomon Islands. Gary said he'd love to go. Joe asked him to come with us, but Gary answered that he couldn't afford it. Then Joe said, "I will pay for it. How much is it Mummy? I have money in my bank."

22 March 2020 Joe wrote me a Mother's Day card:

To Mum xxxx

Mum I know it's hard for you right now but I still love you to the moon and back.

From Joe

Hearts Of Hope Outreach

Chapter 14

The Life We Never Expected

I borrowed this title from a book that a couple wrote, who had two children with severe autism. I am not comparing our family to theirs, but this is probably the most difficult chapter to write in this entire book. I must start the chapter by saying that I do not understand how people navigate the pathways of life without God by their side. In it all, He has been the one that has stuck with us, listening to our cries, bottling up our tears, and whispering, "I understand". When Peter was first placed with us, I was reading the book of Deuteronomy in the Old Testament of the Bible (not one of my favourite books!) and a verse (Deuteronomy 4:20) jumped off the page to me: "But as for you, the Lord took you and brought you out of the iron-smelting furnace, out of Egypt, to be the people of his inheritance, as you now are." I pray this verse over our boys every night.

"The drugs his birth mother was addicted to may have an effect on his future development, and there is a 25% chance he could be affected by his birth father's schizophrenia," the medical adviser informed us before the final decision was made on Peter's placement. However, possibly naively, we believed that all the love and care we would give both boys, would cause nurture to triumph over nature. Plus, we have God on our side, so we weren't going to expect difficulties, we would take one day at a time, and ask for help from others, and in the future if we needed it.

As time has passed, we have learnt that the adoption journey has a language all of its own, and many of its expressions are not understood outside of adoption circles, just like professional jargon can be inaccessible to those outside of the profession. Terms like early trauma, secondary trauma, therapeutic parenting, and blocked care,

are now part of our vocabulary, and have given us a better understanding of the "iron-smelting furnace" in the verse God gave me. Sometimes I see the furnace as the trauma the boys are having to overcome, and sometimes I see it as the work God is doing in our lives through the boys!

Interestingly, the Bible verse that I focused on for 2009 was "My grace is sufficient for you, for my power is made perfect in weakness." (2 Corinthians 12:9) Going from one son to two certainly brought new challenges. In addition, looking back, I say that I don't think Peter ever recovered from us taking Joe into our family. "Well, all children have to adjust to a new baby coming home," people would tell me. But Joe wasn't a baby at thirteen months, and we are talking about two boys that suffer from attachment disorder, due to never bonding with their birth mother. After some years passed, the workers from the Child and Adolescent Mental Health Service (CAMHS) said, that although the boys were birth brothers, it would have been better not to place them together due to their complex needs – hindsight is a wonderful thing!

The other side of the desk

The prospect of sitting on the other side of the desk, being a parent and not a teacher, was a wonderful thing. No more pressure of training children for Standard Assessment Tests (SATS - the English government's measure of primary school children's educational achievement), or trying to give each child in the class the very best you could and convincing the parents that this was what you were doing. However, I soon found that it could be a very uncomfortable place to sit!

Walking up the road to nursery one day with Peter, he piped up, "The trees are moving, Mummy."

"Yes, Darling, why do you think the trees are moving?"

"I don't know."

Any child at his age would have connected the fact that the wind was blowing, but this was an early indication of

Peter's delayed development. He is the youngest in the school year, having an August 30th birthday (the English academic year is 1 September to 31 August), and recognising his social and emotional development delay, two years running I begged the school headteacher to keep him in the year below, but to no avail.

In Peter's Reception Year (four - five year olds) I was called into school by the Special Needs Co-ordinator (SENCO),

"Your son is a problem." This wasn't entirely a surprise – there had been frequent home time reports! Peter would bang his head on the floor when he was frustrated about something, and if he was frustrated with someone else, he couldn't keep his hands to himself! But, my hackles rose (the Mama Bear instinct, protect your children at all costs).

"I know from all my training, that you can say that there *is* a problem, but you never label a child *as* the problem." She looked somewhat taken aback, and on this occasion I felt I had made my point, but there were to be many more meetings at school when I felt like the naughty schoolgirl on the wrong side of the desk!

I always tried to attend parent assembly on a Friday morning. "The star of the week for Green Class goes to Peter. Come along Peter, come and receive your certificate," the headteacher smiled. But the smile turned somewhat frosty, when Peter would not go up and receive his certificate. He lacked confidence, and we didn't know if this was part of his adoption legacy, feeling he wasn't good enough to deserve recognition, but the headteacher definitely lacked understanding. We worked hard to build his confidence, but sometimes you felt as if you were kicking against the goads.

WE ARE HAVING AN EASTER HAT COMPETITION

Please encourage your child to decorate a hat and bring it into school on Friday 26th March. In the afternoon, each class will take part in a parade and the competition will be

judged with a prize for each class. We would like to invite the adults to take part, there will be an adult prize too!

My creative ideas, alongside Gibs' artistic skills, meant that Peter, Joe and I all had our hats ready for the Easter parade. All taking part was a great part of family bonding. Joe's class came into the hall and Joe gave me a little wave when he saw me sitting with the other parents. Then Peter's class came in, but where was Peter? At first I thought that perhaps he had just been delayed, but as the proceedings developed and he still didn't appear my heart sank. I had to get up and parade with about nine other Mums who had made a hat, but I felt mortified knowing that my older son wasn't there. This mortification turned to grief and a measure of anger, when I found out that Peter had been excluded from the event for 'misbehaviour'. This was exactly the type of social experience that Peter needed to have, apart from the fact that I felt I could at least have been forewarned rather than suffer through the event.

"Special"

And this was the prelude of worse to come. At seven years old, Peter began to receive temporary exclusions from school, which disrupted our lives rather than his. Eventually, by the time Peter was in Year 4, the school decided that they couldn't fund the support he needed and suggested that we apply for an Education Health Care Plan (EHCP), with a view to acquiring a place for him at a special school for children with social, emotional and mental health (SEMH) needs. "Special School" definitely has stigma attached to it, but we were despairing about the way forward, so we swallowed our pride – after all, Peter is special. (In God's eyes each and every one of us is uniquely special, and God has given us a deep love for these boys that He has given to us.) The EHCP was granted, and we identified a school that we really liked, but alas, a whole term of Year 5 passed before a place was available. The delay caused a great deal of damage, but in January we were very relieved to see him transfer.

Once the focus at the primary school was taken off Peter, it seemed to move to Joe. We thought we had tackled it all with Peter but incidents with Joe were even more concerning, and we really cried out to God, our strength and sustainer. Joe has no sense of danger, and when something triggered him, he would climb on the windowsills. On one occasion, the staff had to remove all the other children from the classroom for their safety and for Joe's safety. Another time he refused to come home at the end of the school day. This obviously didn't reflect well on us as his parents, until he confided in a trusted teacher that he didn't want to come home to be with Peter. Finally, at the end of the summer term in 2016, as Joe was completing Year 4, he was given a temporary exclusion. The next term was spent taking lessons on his own with support assistants, unable to mix with other children even at playtime. A plan to re-integrate him was never implemented, and despite the valiant efforts of his mentors, his levels of attainment fell.

By January 2017, we realised that Joe was "special" too. The school advised us to put in a parent request for an EHCP for him. There had been a few staff changes at school (sometimes a telling factor of a school environment) and at the meeting, the evidence the school presented looked as if they could meet his needs, and the EHCP request was turned down. We came out of the meeting and I broke down, all the emotional strain of the previous four months washed over me like a torrent. I sobbed to our adoption social worker, "Where do we go now?" He was shocked that the request had been refused, but the member of staff from school was witnessing this, and when she returned to school, they realised their mistake and they put in an appeal. But precious time had been lost.

We had already arranged to take the boys on a trip of a lifetime to the Philippines and then onto the Solomon Islands for two months towards the end of the summer term.

The special school had assured us that they would keep Peter's place open for the September, but Joe's future was unknown. The school's appeal of Joe's EHCP was successful, but the placement meeting didn't take place until the first week in September, when schools were opening again after the long summer break. We wanted Joe to go to the same special school as Peter, but yet again there were no places available. Then the next blow came, his primary school would not take him back on roll whilst we were waiting for a place to become available at the special school. In my mind, it was all rather too convenient for them – they had moved him off their books without having to register another exclusion.

My advocate role came into play. For the first half of the autumn term, every week, I made phone calls and sent e-mails, eventually even contacting our local Member of Parliament (MP), trying to get Joe a school place (a statutory right in England). In the meantime, the special school were realising the complexity of Peter's needs, and the strain the situation was putting on our home. Due to these concerns, they created a place for Joe at the special school after the October half term holiday, thank God for some professionals who have a heart and genuine concern.

Chapter 15

On The Home Front

Managing the behaviour of toddlers, whom you can still scoop up in your arms and pacify, is very different to managing the behaviour of growing boys. Due to their early start, our boys often still react like toddlers. 2014, we are staying in Windsor, whilst Gibs attends a conference in London. Peter, Joe and I have a great day at Lego Land. It was thirsty work, and at the end of the day Peter goes to get a drink at a drinking fountain. Joe decides he wants one too and the boys get into a scuffle. Mother bear here intervenes, trying to separate them. Peter brings his fist up and punches me in the face, giving me a black eye. Shocked, and totally embarrassed by the stares of all the onlookers, I usher the boys to the car, trying to bite back my tears. When we pick up Gibs, I tell him what has happened, and he confronts Peter, who goes into total meltdown. The following day, I took the boys swimming, and Peter announced to a lady in the pool, "I did that to my Mum." He was not gloating, but there was also no remorse, it was as if the consequences of his actions did not connect with his emotions. This has been borne out in the last couple of years, when Peter was diagnosed with Foetal Alcohol Syndrome Disorders (FASDs), a symptom of which is the inability to understand consequences.

Distant shores

Our extended stay in the Happy Isles (the Solomon Islands are known as this) in the summer of 2017, let our boys experience a different life, especially as they spent some time in Gibs' village, whilst we did some charity work in the main town. Peter stayed in Uncle Reuben's house, and Joe stayed across the road in Aunty Esther's house – separation helps their relationship! Extended family is very important to Peter, he will often ask when he can see his cousins in the Solomon Islands again.

The sun rises at 6am and sets at 6pm 365 days a year, and the children are up and around as the sun rises, and have a freedom that is not safe in our society today. Our boys thought this was great. They ran around bare foot (with faithful aunts applying sun tan lotion and mosquito repellant), climbed trees, swam in the sea, and went fishing in the canoe with their uncle. The outdoor life suits them, and thankfully access to technology is much more limited. Could this be an environment where they could thrive?

The shared pain of trauma

The whole journey of understanding early trauma, the separation from birth parents whatever the circumstances, is a painful one, and one that has heard me cry out to God for a spirit of wisdom and understanding. I was driving Joe home from his short break at Yorkshire Camps and he had his headphones on absorbed in his music as usual. Suddenly, he dislodged the headphones and said to me, "This song is like my life, Mum."

"Why Joe, what does the song say?"

To make sure I got it, he repeated the phrases to me, rather than expecting me to decipher the words in the song: "I'm trapped in my bedroom with my guilt up to the ceiling," and "I feel I should be punished, but I never learn my lesson." He started to sob, in great convulsions. I started to cry too, not the safest of behaviours whilst driving, but this was a window into his heart, and his pain was tangible.

It didn't stop there. The song went on to speak of the mum passing and the singer realising she would no longer be part of his life. Trying to bring some comfort or security, I said, "I haven't passed, Joe."

"But you will."

"Not until you have others in your life, just like Dad and I do now that our Mums and Dads have passed. We love you

Joe," then I continued, trying to address the guilt, "And God loves us all so much. He forgives us whatever we do, as long as we are genuinely sorry." This seemed to pacify him at the time, but it also left me wondering what other struggles were occupying his young mind, plus it spurred me to pray for our boys even more fervently, they are facing battles way beyond anything either of us had experienced.

Dixon of Dock Green and Z Cars

My only experience of uniformed police came from watching these two TV series in the 1960s and 1970s! But the onset of puberty for Peter, and then Joe, exacerbated the challenges. Social Care had established that we were dealing with child to parent violence, rather than parent to child violence, and in a sense this was a relief. The school parent support worker rang, "Sally, you must start involving the police. Peter's behaviours are becoming more dangerous, both towards you and to himself."

The first time of ringing 999 (English police emergency number) felt unreal, but it became a regular occurrence, to the extent that when the officers attend our house now, one of them has usually been before! We have nothing but praise for the police, they show great understanding of the boys' needs, and also try to support us in any way they can to meet those needs.

On one occasion, Peter was cross with me about something (I can't remember what it was on that occasion), and he picked up a recycling bag and threw it at me. It had a jar inside and it hit me above the eye. I crumpled and cried out, and Gibs came running. He took one look at me (bleeding) and said, "What have you done, Peter?" Peter kicked the wall and ran out of the house. We rang 999. The police arrived and drove off up the road to find him. They took him into custody. I was in emotional turmoil, shock from the injury (which fortunately hadn't done any permanent damage), but also worried about our son being taken into custody. The police brought Peter back later in the evening and his bizarre comments reflected the state of his mental health: "Sorry Mum, I didn't know there was a jar in the bag." Then to his Dad, "There was a bed in the cell Dad and it was really comfortable." Back to me, "They gave me two drinks of hot chocolate Mum, why were they so kind to me?"

"In the day of trouble he will keep me safe" (Psalm 27:5)

It was late afternoon on a pleasant summer's day and a builder had come to give me a quote to build a side wall in the garden. He seemed to be a good guy, advising me on the best and most economical way to have it done, when two police officers appeared, interrupting our conversation.

"Are you the mother of Joe?"

"Yes I am, what has he done?"

"He's come off his bike riding down Churwell Hill."

"Is he OK?"

"I think we better go inside" (at this point the builder beat a hasty retreat, telling me he would be in touch).

We went into the kitchen, where Gibs joined us, "What's going on?" I quickly explained that Gibs was my husband, Joe's Dad, and the officer continued: "Joe has gone over the handlebars of his bike and hit his head on the road. The ambulance is with him and the paramedics need one of you to accompany him to hospital." As bile filled my mouth, my brain went into overdrive.

"Darling, you had better go to him, as if he needs bringing back from the hospital, I would need to go and pick him up, as you can't drive."

Gibs agreed and duly set off with the police officers in their car, and I started the sickening waiting. It was one of those times when minutes feel like hours, but eventually my phone buzzed. I opened my Whatsapp as if my life depended on it, only to find photos of Joe in a neck brace and totally immobilised. My heart was racing as I tried to ring Gibs, willing him to pick up, even though I didn't know if he would have reception in the hospital. I don't know how much more time passed, it felt like an eternity, before Gibs' name flashed up on my screen. I gave up any pretence of calm, and like someone gasping for their last breath, I questioned him, "What's going on. How is he?"

"It's OK Darling, they have done a full body X-ray and nothing is broken. They are just concerned about the possibility of internal injuries, so they are keeping him under observation."

What Gibs was telling me weighed heavy on me, I don't think he understood that internal injuries could be more serious than broken bones. "Tell him I love him," I said, "And please keep me informed." As we ended the call, I sank to my knees, "Please Father, you promise to keep your children safe. Put your healing hand upon Joe now and let him come out of this unscathed." I texted Mum Barbara and Dad John, briefly explaining to them what had happened and asking them to pray. Not only was I concerned for Joe, but I was deeply missing Gibs' reassuring presence, this was the sort of thing we needed to face together, I felt very alone.

Later in the evening, Gibs rang again, "They want to keep him in overnight, and he wants you." After a short explanation to Peter, a very kind friend, whom we had tried to support through a tragic circumstance, took me to the hospital, as I wasn't sure where to park overnight. Gibs and I did a quick exchange at the hospital and the friend took him home to Peter. I went in to see Joe. He looked very vulnerable lying in the hospital bed, with scrapes and bruises, and he reached out to take my hand, "My wheel hit a bump in the road Mum, and when I hit the road everything went black. I wanted you."

"I'm here now, son, and we are praying everything will be alright."

The nurses were wonderful and gave us a room to ourselves, with a camp bed for me. We didn't get much sleep as they needed to come and check his vital statistics every couple of hours, but in the morning, apart from some aches and pains, he didn't seem the worse for wear. They did further checks and another x-ray, then said he could be discharged with no follow up needed. However, before letting him go, the nurse in charge gave him a stern warning: "Joe, do you realise how lucky you are? We've had children come in here who have had bike accidents, and like you, weren't wearing a helmet, and they didn't walk out of the hospital. It is vital that you wear a bike helmet."

I wish I could say that he heeded their warning, but as is Joe's norm, the blame for the accident lay in the fact that the road was faulty. He is unable to accept responsibility, and the only thing that changed, was that he wouldn't ride down Churwell Hill again. For our part, we were grateful yet again for the prayers of those who love and support us.

"He has delivered us from such a deadly peril, and he will deliver us again. On him we have set our hope that he will continue to deliver us, as you help us by your prayers." (2 Corinthians 1:10-11)

AWOL (Absent WithOut Leave)

"I'm not eating the rest of this," Joe called to me as he jumped up from the table, where he had sat down to eat his meal, having finally come in late in the afternoon. "But it's your favourite, Joe, spaghetti and meatballs," I responded to no avail, as he ran out the front door laughing. It was Saturday and he had been out since lunchtime, playing with a boy in his class, who has a dubious influence on him. At least he was out and not glued to his phone. But as the evening wore on, it started to get dark and Joe hadn't come home. We rang his mobile phone, but no reply. We rang the other boy's mum, he wasn't home either.

As time rolled on, we became more and more concerned. God does promise that he gives his angels to guard us (Psalm 91:11), but he also helps those who help themselves, expecting us to act responsibly. So, we drove around the places they frequented, but at 10.15 pm, when there was still no sign of them, we rang the police to report them missing. Having done everything we could do practically, we did the only other thing we knew to do, we joined hands and we prayed: "Father God, wherever our son is now, please keep him safe, and help him to come home." I'd love to tell you that having prayed, we rested in peace, but that wouldn't be quite true.

The police visited to take details and tried to be reassuring – they were probably used to teenagers not coming home, but we weren't! So as the night wore on, we sat together, willing my mobile to ring. Gibs was distractedly flicking through his Facebook posts, whilst in my mind I was going through every scenario of where Joe could possibly be, and perhaps worse, what could possibly have happened to him.

"How could he be so selfish, putting us through this?" fumed Gibs. "What if he's got himself into serious trouble? *What* is he thinking of?"

Midnight came and went. No news. Another mug of decaf tea each, although by this time we could each have done with a good shot of caffeine to keep us awake. I tried to read a magazine, nervously flicking the pages whilst being aware I hadn't absorbed a thing…

1 a.m. Sunday morning came and went. We spoke little, and eventually the physical and emotional weariness overtook us, and we dozed fitfully – perhaps the worst thing to do, as your mind starts to play tricks on you.

Finally, just after 2, I was jolted awake as the phone rang. What a relief! The police had found the boys. Gibs turned to me and said, "He's still a young lad. I hope he doesn't have to learn too many lessons the hard way!" Having gone through the whole range of emotions, Gibs had worked through the anger of the stress Joe had put us through and come to the tremendous sense of relief that he had been found safe and sound.

Twenty minutes later, the doorbell rang. There in front of us was Joe, shivering, and looking sorry for himself. This was his story: "We went to Elland Road football ground (Leeds United's ground) to see the memorial to a class friend of ours who died. Then a man, all in black with a black mask, followed us. We made our way to the Porsche garage and tried the doors of the cars on the forecourt. One of them opened so we got in to keep safe. We found the alarm button and we rang the police." The police matched the call to our missing persons reports and picked the boys up!

Our trusting in God hadn't spared us an anxious night. But our hearts had been softened towards Joe, so that when he arrived home, this teenager even allowed me to take him in my arms and hug him, then make him a mug of hot chocolate as we settled him into bed.

Hope

"And now we have run into his heart to hide ourselves in his faithfulness. This is where we find his strength and comfort, for he empowers us to seize what has already been established ahead of time – an unshakable hope! We have this certain hope like a strong anchor holding our souls to God himself." (Hebrews 6:18-19)

So I end this chapter as I started it, because of God's faithfulness, we will make it through. God is our anchor, individually and as a couple, and we have hope for the boys for the future. But we will not only make it through, we will continue, as Jesus promised, "I have come that they might have life, and have it to the full" (John 10:10). We count our blessings, of which there are many. Celebrations play a big part in our lives, and our different cultures seem to blend together to make these highly colourful occasions. Visitors to our Facebook pages often see us embracing new experiences. Pictures of Gibs and my stay in Berlin, visiting incredible scenes from history. Then this last winter, the simple fun of tandem sled rides in the snow in the fields near our house. And there is so much more life to live...

Chapter 16

Transition

Variety is the spice of life!

A printing firm; a sandwich making business; Fox's Biscuit factory; a school kitchen; a care home for the elderly – Gibs undertook roles in all of these settings over the years. He certainly isn't shy of putting his nose to the grindstone. However, his greatest love is his artwork and he set up his own business, SolArt, on a self-employed basis. They say beauty is in the eye of the beholder, and in my eye, not only is he beautiful, but so is his artwork, full of the colour and vibrancy of his Pacific roots. Many of his paintings are collages of flowers or sea life, but not in the abstract form that I personally still struggle to understand and appreciate. At the end of his college art foundation course, there was an exhibition of all the students' work. I stood for a while pondering a 'sculpture', which had been awarded a distinction. It appeared to be a chair, with a rope attached and a bucket hanging from it. Art is definitely an area where it must be said, "Each to his own taste"!

For a season, he was also part of a partnership doing painting and decorating. His fine motor skills and his eye for detail were a great asset in this business, but then a friend raised a concern after Gibs had done some work for him: "Gibs, there are patches of shades of colour on the walls, can you give them another coat of paint, please?" We went together to investigate, and I realised he couldn't see the subtle shades, a consequence of his Ushers disease. Added to this, the fact that he was not now allowed to drive on medical grounds, brought an end to that line of work.

"Parenting is the hardest job in the world" – yes, right up there with brain surgeon and bomb disposal technician. That's why, if you haven't realised it thus far in our story, I am full of admiration for this man I get to call my husband. His most important role to date, was to be the main carer for our boys. Even in our day and age, it takes real humility for a man to be the stay at home parent, whilst his wife goes out and earns the money. Plus, in Gibs' culture, there is always a house girl (usually a young relative) on hand to help with the day-to-day childcare and tasks. In later years, my working hours were more flexible, but we were advised that both of us needed to be at home when our boys were not at school, due to their complex needs.

…and – for me!

"Sally, would you consider coming to work for us as our personal assistant (PA)?" Much to my surprise, the Pastors of our church asked me this whilst I was managing a Sure Start programme in Leeds. It felt like a great honour to be asked to serve in this way, but a lot of negotiation was needed, as it was only a part-time position and the salary offer was much lower. As usual, God came up with the goods. When I discussed the possibility with my Sure Start Manager, he suggested that we ask the board if my post could change to a job share, and they agreed – plus the church went some way to meeting the potential salary gap.

Are there people in your life that you would like to emulate, but you feel you fall far short of? My dear friend Pam is one of these people for me. Pam was working for our church as our centre manager for the charity Christians Against Poverty (CAP – a charity that helps people get out of debt). She is the most amazing lady, full of love and compassion, who hears God for people and shares her love of Jesus with them. Whilst I was working as PA, I was excited to accompany Pam on a few of her visits as a 'befriender' – this is someone who offers friendship to people as the centre manager guides them in their journey out of debt. In 2009, Pam was asked to take on a role in CAP's head office, creating a vacancy for a centre manager in our church. Could I do that role? I decided to apply and I was delighted when I was successful in the application process, but also apprehensive, with the "Follow Pam" tag, as I wasn't the only one who held her in high esteem.

For me, it was the best job that I have done in my working life (and there have been a few!). It is a fantastic charity to work for. And to be invited into people's homes and have them share their lives with you, trusting you with information about some very difficult situations, was an incredible privilege. It was such a joy to see some people work so hard to become debt free and to enjoy the freedom it brought them. It was an even greater joy to see some people come to know Jesus in the way that I know him.

"We have decided that we need a qualified social worker to lead the programme, not a qualified teacher. Therefore you no longer meet the requirements of the post, so we are making you redundant," the Sure Start Board announced to me. Personally, I wonder if they had second thoughts about the job share, but for me this just raised the question, what else did God have in store for me? In time, it became clear. I took on extra days working for the church as the finance officer, taking the administration side in my stride, but finding balancing the books more stressful.

Changing seasons

Looking after our Pastor's four children whilst they were away proved to be good experience for our future even though we didn't know it at the time. This was one of the many ways we served in the church over the years. One of Gibs' early contributions was as a member of the worship team playing his guitar, which he really enjoyed. However, once we had both boys, he made the sacrifice of coming out of the worship team to support me with the boys at church. We started the international ministry together; led small groups; spoke on Sunday mornings; served in many practical areas; and were part of the leadership team of the church. But as the years passed, the boys became more challenging, and we decided we had to step back. We made the decision to come out of the leadership team. My role as centre manager for CAP was a time-consuming role and became my major focus of serving. Gibs would sometimes accompany me on visits as a befriender if I were visiting a male.

Are we in the right place?

"Are you thinking of taking up a role at CAP head office, or of retiring?" the Pastor asked me. It seemed only a casual question, but as the next few months passed it nagged ever more persistently. Finally I had the opportunity to follow up with him: "Why did you ask me that question?" In the discussion that followed, it became clear that our coming out of the leadership team had a consequence I hadn't foreseen. There seemed to be a desire for each of the major ministry areas to be headed up by a leader, so that the whole of the church could move in step. As I mulled this over, I became increasingly doubtful about how appropriate it was for me to continue as CAP centre manager, and therefore felt unsettled.

This led to me taking the situation to God. When you decide to accept what Jesus did for you on the cross and give your life to God, he promises to give you the person of his Holy Spirit, to be alongside you. Over the next few months, I felt I heard the Holy Spirit speak to me through a quiet inner voice. The first time, was when I was telling God that I felt unsettled, and sensed that his reply was, "What if I am unsettling you?" Sometimes it is so much easier to stay in your comfort zone.

I had taken on a second role with CAP as a speaker at some of their regional events, and in January 2018, a team of us attended a national conference. One of the speakers shared that if you don't have the right people on team, it can cap your growth. You all need to share the same culture, DNA, and vision. Gibs and I needed to ask ourselves if we were in the right place, as the last thing we wanted to do was to cap the church growth.

God continued to highlight things to me in his word, the Bible. I knew he was up to something, and by the beginning of March, I was challenged as to what good seed had to die in my life for me to be more fruitful. (1 Corinthians 15:36).

"Gibs, I believe that God is challenging me to give up my CAP centre manager work. What do you think, Darling? It would be a big step, as it is our main source of income."

"If God is telling you to do it Sally, he will provide for our needs. We just need to trust him."

Stepping out of the boat

"'Lord, if it's you,' Peter replied, 'tell me to come to you on the water.'

'Come,' Jesus said.

Then Peter got down out of the boat, walked on the water and came towards Jesus." (Matthew 14:28-29)

This is an extraordinary story in the Bible, where Peter, Jesus' disciple, walks on the water.

God's next prompting to me was that I needed to get out of the boat, just like Peter did. I started to reflect on the story and imagined that there would have been many voices in the boat around Peter, and I named the voices:

Mr Play It Safe "Peter, just stay in the boat, Jesus is coming to us."

Mr Doubter "Peter, it might not really be Jesus, and you might drown."

Mr Jealous "Why do you always have to be the doer Peter, think you're better than everyone else?"

Mr Discourager "Look Peter, here comes another big wave!"

Mr Encourager "You can do it Peter, keep your eyes upon Jesus."

I knew we would have to be careful what voices we listened to. Peter only started to sink when he took his eyes off Jesus and let fear come in. But he was the only one who experienced the miracle of walking on the water, and when he did start to sink, Jesus reached out his hand and caught him. Our whole lives to date had been a Fantastic Adventure In Trusting Him (FAITH), and we didn't ever want the adventure to stop. So, with Gibs' agreement, I took the big step of faith and told the Pastors that I was resigning my CAP role.

As Gibs and I continued to talk about the future, we began to realise that the resigning of my CAP role released this ministry to someone else to lead, and signalled the time for us to move on from the church. This was a massive decision, especially for me, as I had known Pastors Ian and Julie for over thirty years, and their family was like my family. It was difficult telling them of our decision, as they had invested so much into our lives over the years, but they released us with their blessing and the church gave us a very generous gift of two short breaks to thank us for all our input over the years.

However, we knew that God was repositioning us, even though we didn't know where to! There is a story in the Old Testament of the Bible, where God tells a man called Abram to leave his land and go to a new land (Genesis 12:1). He obeys and pitches his tent at the edge of vast plains. Abram didn't know what lay ahead, but the vastness was full of God possibilities.

Next steps?

"Develop a passion for learning, if you do, you will never cease to grow." (Anthony J. D'Angelo). Bearing this in mind, I trained as a life coach. I thought it would give me another string to my bow, but I also knew that it wouldn't bring in the necessary income in the near future. Hence, with great excitement, I announced to Gibs,

"I have an interview." But the day before the interview, we had an appointment with our financial adviser, who had been looking into my pensions for me.

"Sally, you have a good teacher's pension, as well as two other smaller ones. You don't need to work if you don't want to."

"How long can I draw my pension for?"

"For the rest of your life," came the reply.

I was amazed.

The interview went well, and two days later I received the call with the result.

"Sally, you had an excellent interview, but we think you are more suited to a face-to-face role, rather than this management role which is more office-based, so we are not offering you the job." Disappointment? No, relief, now that I knew we were set up financially to explore what God had for us.

"No man is an island, entire of itself; every man is a piece of the continent, a part of the main." These words of John Donne, reflect the biblical truth, that we are all parts of one body, of which Christ is the head (1 Corinthians 12:27). We believe this is also why the Bible tells us not to give up meeting together (Hebrews 10:25), so as we moved on, Gibs and I needed to find a new church family. Just as families come in all shapes and sizes, so do churches, the same Bible based Christian doctrine, but different make-ups and styles of worship. We found our new spiritual home at Bridge Community Church (BCC) in Leeds. With over seventy nations represented, and a great children's and youth ministry, it felt like the best fit for us.

As is our wont, we threw ourselves into the life of Bridge Community Church and volunteered in different capacities. In 2019, after meeting some international students who didn't have connections in the church, we launched an international students' group, as we felt our personal experiences equipped us to offer them friendship and support. Gibs also met someone at the church who introduced him to a group of people who go out onto the streets of Leeds to share the good news of Jesus. His eyes light up as he tells me with that enthusiasm I love to see, "Sally, an English lady helped to pioneer the sharing of the gospel on my Island in the mid 1800s, and now I get to share it here in England. As I speak, I can feel the power of God flowing through me, and I long for people here to know the incredible love of God."

Other shores?

Kimnel Hall Conference Centre in the 1980s, I can still vividly remember the speaker's words: "There are hundreds of children suffering with AIDS in Africa, who will go to help them?" I went back to my bedroom and sobbed on my knees, "Please God, don't ask me to go as a missionary to Africa to help the AIDS children." It wasn't the fear of AIDS that fuelled my cry, but my mental image of a missionary as an old fashioned spinster! However, the speaker's appeal had sown a seed in my heart to serve people in another country, and this seed grew over the years. Going out to the Solomon Islands with VSO was part of fulfilling this, and of course, it was also the case, that if it wasn't for the political coup, Gibs and I had intended to stay in the Solomon Islands as I continued volunteering for VSO.

In 2017 we put a toe in the water to see if our future as a family lay in another country, by our trip of a lifetime to the Philippines and the Solomon Islands to do charity work. Gibs and I loved helping the charity "Hearts Of Hope", although we had some concerns about their accountability. There are many advantages to life in the Solomons, some of which the boys appreciated more than others. Life is much simpler, and certainly less ruled by technology, plus there is much more time spent in the outdoors. So, whilst we were there, we collected the papers to apply for visas, to look at the possibility of moving to the Solomon Islands long term. But as Gibs is now a British Citizen, we found out that we would have to have sponsorship, and if we wanted to work, we would have to prove that we were doing work that Solomon Islanders couldn't do. Was this a closed door?

Chapter 17

Into The Future

Can we do this?

"We don't know if we can meet Peter's needs any longer, he may have to go back into care." Gibs was broken as he told this via Facebook Messenger to his adult nephew Joshua in the Solomon Islands. Joshua relayed this information to Gibs' sister Esther, and the response came back: "My Mum is really upset. She says Peter is part of our wider family, and he can't go back into care, she would be happy to look after him here in the Solomon Islands." I cried. This was our family on the other side of the world sharing our love for our boys. But we were no nearer a possible move to the Solomon Islands. Not until we were invited, along with other Islanders, to London for the setting in of the Solomon Islands' High Commissioner in May 2018. "We are putting a dual citizenship law before parliament this July," the Solomon Islands Prime Minister announced. I cheered out loud, much to the amusement of the Islanders gathered there. Incredibly, later in the event, I had an opportunity to speak to the Prime Minister about offering life coaching in the Solomon Islands and his response was very positive. Dual citizenship would open a window for us to go and live in the Solomon Islands for a couple of years, the plan being that we would live on the main island and Peter would stay with Gibs' family and go to school on their island, then we would all be reunited in school holidays.

The wheels of motion move very slowly in the Solomon Islands, so it was December 2018 before we heard that the bill had finally been put to their parliament. Our excitement grew, but we were getting ahead of the Solomon Island's system! Even when it passed through parliament, it still had to be approved by the Governor General, and this seemed to take an eternity. Finally, the guidance was available, but alas, it wasn't what we expected. It seems to require someone to have been living in the Solomon Islands for five years previous to applying for dual citizenship. "We need to go Gibs, and ask the questions directly, it is so difficult to get answers through e-mails and Facebook Messenger."

The gift of marriage

"SPECIAL OFFER – If you have qualified as a life coach, I am offering you the Marriage Coaching training at a discounted rate. This training will help you improve your marriage, as well as equip you to enrich the marriages of others."

Sadly, we had heard that Gibs' niece's marriage, that we had attended in the Solomon Islands in 2017, had run into trouble. Possibly even sadder in our eyes, was the fact that we found out through her angry posts on Facebook. "Is there anyone who will help them over there Gibs, is there any relationship counselling?"

"The parents will try and sort it out, Sally. If her husband has betrayed her, he will be expected to pay compensation."

"But that won't help them with their relationship Gibs, will it? Is it just accepted that the marriage is over, or will someone try to help them to rebuild their relationship?"

"I don't know, Sally."

This weighed heavy on our hearts, and it coincided with the discounted offer of marriage coaching, so we decided to do the course together. For us, our marriage is such a gift, that we want to help others to also enjoy their marriage, whether here in England, or anywhere else.

Following the completion of the course, I enquired of the trainer, "Has anyone used the materials to write a course for couples?"

"No," she responded, "but you could be the one to do it!"

Never being one to turn down a challenge, I took up the baton and wrote a marriage enrichment course. Imagine our delight when we met with the Senior Pastor of our church and he encouraged us about the need for such a course in the church. He then read and endorsed the materials and we advertised our first course in the church. We were overwhelmed when fifteen couples booked onto the course, and what a joy it was to share what we have learnt and are learning as we continue to build our relationship together.

What does tomorrow hold?

Horoscopes, clairvoyants, fortune tellers, people have an irresistible urge to know what the future holds, but I for one am glad that I can't see into the future. I am not sure how I would have coped with knowing that I wouldn't meet my husband till I was in my forties, but I am pleased now that I lived my single years to the full. The Bible offers two different perspectives on this, "Do not worry about tomorrow, for tomorrow will worry about itself. Each day has enough trouble of its own," (Matthew 6 34), and "Do not boast about tomorrow, for you do not know what a day may bring." (Proverbs 27:1). Worrying about what might happen tomorrow, and boasting about what you will achieve tomorrow, are both futile, when you have limited control over the future.

How many of us would have coped with knowing that a global pandemic was on the way, and if we did know, how could we have prepared ourselves for it? Sadly, many have learnt that each day has enough trouble of its own, and we have all learnt that we cannot 'boast' about our plans for tomorrow, as the pandemic, along with government guidelines, may curtail them.

Lockdown

March 2020 brought the first lockdown here in England, and the announcement that schools would close. My teaching background kicked in and I was proud of the daily timetable I had worked out for the boys – short work periods on essential subjects such as English and maths, interspersed with practical sessions, such as time playing an instrument with Dad for Peter and building lego models or cooking with me for Joe. It worked for all of two days, and by the end of day two I was tearing my hair out and abandoned the plan! Being 'special' (having special educational needs), became our passport to sanity – God bless Boris (English prime minister) for declaring that school provision should be made for children of key workers and children with special educational needs. Each boy was offered two days a week in the first lockdown, different days to each other in order to minimise the conflict between them at home. In the second lockdown in September 2020, we confessed to being 'extremely vulnerable' and both boys were given a phased return to full time schooling.

"No Peter, you can't have your friends in the house," and "No Joe, you can't go out and hang out with your friends. We are in lockdown because of corona virus and we cannot mix with other people because we all need to keep safe." But how do you keep a twelve and thirteen year old in the house if they are determined to go out? I have to admit there were times when we didn't manage it, especially when peers came knocking at the door with total disregard for the regulations. We are so very grateful that none of us has suffered from Covid, nor have we lost anyone close to us. We have constantly claimed God's protection, and I have a sneaky suspicion that God knows that a Covid case could have been the straw that broke the camel's back.

Some of you might think that God doesn't work in that way, but this is how the Bible puts it: "We all experience times of testing, which is normal for every human being. But God will be faithful to you. He will screen and filter the severity, nature, and timing of every test or trial you face so that you can bear it. And each test is an opportunity to trust him more, for along with every trial God has provided for you a way of escape that will bring you out of it victoriously." (1 Corinthians 10:13) God knows how much we can bear and he won't let us get to breaking point.

"People are more important than things." (Randy Pousch).

This is certainly true for Gibs and I, but suddenly lockdown closed all the outlets: no more preaching on the streets for Gibs; no more giving hospitality in our home; no more volunteering at the church toddler group, or at the church cafe for me; and the last couple of sessions of the marriage enrichment course had to be conducted on Zoom, certainly not the interaction we had been enjoying. We were aware how many people were alone, or isolated, so how could we keep up contact with people and let people know that they are not alone? Creative ideas were needed.

"I don't like cooking," our 89 year old bachelor neighbour told me over the garden fence one day. So I consulted with Gibs, the head cook, "Gibs, Alf says he doesn't like cooking. We cook for four of us, so shall we make it five and offer to give him a meal each day?"

"Of course, Sally," and so it was that we started passing him a meal over the wall each day. This simple act opened up lots of contact and support between us. When I took him for his Covid vaccine in January 2021, I was offered mine at the same time, so I got in early on his ticket! This interaction has culminated recently in him accompanying us to church on Sundays, and each week he tells us, "I am looking forward to going to the concert with you on Sunday"!

Five A Day – oh yes, we try to get our five fruit and veg each day, but this was different. I had the idea of working through my contacts list, both my phone book and my Facebook contacts, ringing, or sending an encouraging message to five people each day and asking if they had any specific prayer needs. It was great, as I connected with people near and far, some living on our estate, and others I hadn't connected with personally for years, like my youth leader from my teens, who is now in his 80s. Such a joy too to share in people's prayer requests, and brilliant when they came back to me with the answer: "My daughter has a job Sally, thank you so much for standing with us."

All this time

"What will we do with all this time, now that most of our activities are curtailed?"

Gibs started writing songs, many of them using words from the Bible following in the footsteps of King David, who wrote the Psalms in the Old Testament. Most days the house is filled with the sound of his guitar playing and songs, and sometimes I do a sneaky little dance when nobody else is watching (especially not the boys, who would not appreciate this "granny" strutting her stuff!), to bring a smile to Gibs' face. He is set to record a number of his songs for a second album, once he and his friends can get together safely to do the recording. For my part, I felt spurred on to write our story, and we have spent happy hours as we have discovered more and more of each others' stories, which we hope you have enjoyed reading.

Money saved from staying at home was ploughed into improvement work in our house and garden. Despite not having green fingers, I have found incredible pleasure in seeing flowers flourish and bloom. It feels like an ideal time to put our house on the market ready to make a major move to the Solomon Islands, but of course we can't even visit the Islands at this time. Now we are focusing on saving for when we can next make the trip, so that we can try to get Gibs' Solomon Islands' passport renewed to aid us on the dual citizenship journey. We do not know what the future holds, but we are confident that it is in God's hands. So I finish our story by reminding you of the words of a song from my youth days that I quoted in an earlier chapter:

"I know who holds the future and he guides me with his hand

With God things don't just happen, everything by him is planned

So as I face tomorrow with its problems large and small

I'll trust the God of miracles, give to him my all."

We are two ordinary people, who have lived extraordinary lives to date, through an extraordinary God, and have enjoyed the thrill of the ride, so our closing statement is this:

"As for me and my family, we will serve the Lord." (Joshua 24:15).

Gibs at The British Museum to present his paintings

Gib's album 'Orphan Boy'

Epilogue

The Invitation

A love like this

Who wouldn't want to know a love like this?
A love that does not wax or wane
A love that does not have moods
A love that forgives and forgets
A love that believes the best of you
A love that wants the best for you
A love that has the power to deliver the best for you
A love so deep that He gave his only Son to die for you
A love that He longs to lavish upon you

Our story

We hope that you have enjoyed our story. It is a testimony of this love, the love of God that exceeds all other loves. Our greatest joy would be for you to know this love in the way that we have come to know it. If you would like to accept the offer of Father God to come into a personal relationship with him, and to know his love from now into eternity, we invite you to say this prayer:

A prayer

Father God, thank you for giving your Son Jesus to die on the cross for me

Please forgive me for everything I have said or done wrong, and for going my own way

I ask you Jesus to come into my life and give me a new start

I choose to make you the Boss of my life

I ask you to give me the gift of your Holy Spirit to help me to live for you

And to reveal Father God's love to me more and more each day

Amen

Your new life

If you have said that prayer sincerely, you can now know God in a personal way as your Father. Please tell someone about your decision, as you are like a new baby in Christ and you will need the help and support of others. Talk to God as your Father about everything and anything, and listen to him, this is prayer. Start to read his word, the Bible. There are good easy to read versions, and there are helpful daily Bible notes. Look for a church where people have a personal relationship with Jesus, and where you feel comfortable with their style of worship.

Contact

If you have questions, or you need encouragement, please e-mail us at sallypben@gmail.com, putting "The Thrill of the Ride" in the subject line.